Books by Rich Westcott

The Phillies Encyclopedia (with Frank Bilovsky)
Diamond Greats
The New Phillies Encyclopedia (with Frank Bilovsky)
Phillies '93—An Incredible Season
Philadelphia's Old Ballparks
Mike Schmidt
Masters of the Diamond
No-Hitters—The 225 Games, 1893–1999 (with Allen Lewis)
Splendor on the Diamond
Great Home Runs of the 20th Century
A Century of Philadelphia Sports

Winningest Pitchers

Winningest Pitchers

Baseball's 300-Game Winners

Rich Westcott

 Temple University Press

Philadelphia

Temple University Press, Philadelphia 19122
Copyright © 2002 by Temple University
All rights reserved
Published 2002
Printed in the United States of America

Library of Congress Cataloging-in-Publication Data

Westcott, Rich.
  Winningest pitchers : baseball's 300-game winners / Rich Westcott.
    p. cm.
  Includes bibliographical references (p.)
  ISBN 1-56639-949-1 (pbk. : alk. paper)
    1. Pitchers (Baseball)—United States—Biography. I. Title.
  GV865.A1 W476 2002
  796.357'092'2—dc21
  [B]

                                        2001054249

To Erica and Rachel,

two wonderful and very special little girls

Contents

Introduction   xiii

Pud Galvin   1
The First 300-Game Winner

Tim Keefe   9
Strong Will Prevails

Mickey Welch   17
A Lot to Smile About

Old Hoss Radbourn   25
Never Too Tired to Pitch

John Clarkson   33
Thriving on Praise

Kid Nichols   41
No Decade More Dazzling

Cy Young   49
An Unapproachable Record

Christy Mathewson   59
Idol of the Masses

Eddie Plank   69
A Hitter's Nightmare

Walter Johnson   77
Fastball Was Fearsome

Grover Cleveland Alexander   87
From Triumph to Tragedy

Lefty Grove   97
Hot-Tempered Fireballer

Warren Spahn   107
The Complete Package

Early Wynn   117
Expert in Intimidation

Gaylord Perry   127
Master of Mind Games

Steve Carlton   137
No Distractions Allowed

Tom Seaver   147
Artist on the Mound

Phil Niekro   157
King of the Knuckleballers

Don Sutton   167
Never Missed a Turn

Nolan Ryan   177
Strikeout Specialist

Are 300-Game Winners a Vanishing Breed?   187

Photo Credits   195

About the Author   197

300-Game Winners

Date	Pitcher	Age	Team	Opponent	Score	Career Record
Oct. 5, 1888	Pud Galvin	31	Pittsburgh (NL)	Washington	5–1	361–308
June 4, 1890	Tim Keefe	33	New York (PL)	Boston	9–4	342–225
July 28, 1890	Mickey Welch	31	New York (NL)	Pittsburgh	4–2	307–210
June 2, 1891	Old Hoss Radbourn	36	Cincinnati (NL)	Boston	10–8	309–195
Sept. 21, 1892	John Clarkson	31	Cleveland (NL)	Pittsburgh	3–2	328–178
July 7, 1900	Kid Nichols	30	Boston (NL)	Chicago	11–4	361–208
July 12, 1901	Cy Young	34	Boston (AL)	Philadelphia	5–3	511–316
June 13, 1912	Christy Mathewson	32	New York (NL)	Chicago	3–2	373–188
Aug. 28, 1915	Eddie Plank	39	St. Louis (FL)	Kansas City	3–2	327–194
May 14, 1920	Walter Johnson	32	Washington (AL)	Detroit	9–8	417–279
Sept. 20, 1924	Grover C. Alexander	37	Chicago (NL)	New York	7–3	373–208
July 25, 1941	Lefty Grove	41	Boston (AL)	Cleveland	10–6	300–141
Aug. 11, 1961	Warren Spahn	40	Milwaukee (NL)	Chicago	2–1	363–245
July 13, 1963	Early Wynn	43	Cleveland (AL)	Kansas City	7–4	300–244
May 6, 1982	Gaylord Perry	43	Seattle (AL)	New York	7–3	314–265
Sept. 23, 1983	Steve Carlton	38	Philadelphia (NL)	St. Louis	6–2	329–244
Aug. 4, 1985	Tom Seaver	40	Chicago (AL)	New York	4–1	311–205
Oct. 6, 1985	Phil Niekro	46	New York (AL)	Toronto	8–0	318–274
June 18, 1986	Don Sutton	41	California (AL)	Texas	5–1	324–256
July 31, 1990	Nolan Ryan	43	Texas (AL)	Milwaukee	11–3	324–292

Introduction

Since major league baseball began, more than 12,000 pitchers have trudged to the mound to face opposing batters. Some have performed successfully; some have not. Of the entire pitching population, however, just 20 hurlers have reached the ultimate goal of their profession.

These 20 form one of the most elite groups not only in baseball but in all of sports. They are major league baseball's 300-game winners.

Being the winning pitcher in 300 games is an achievement that extends far beyond ordinary levels of performance. It is a feat that only the best, the most durable, and the most courageous hurlers attain. The accomplishment requires diligence, perseverance, innovation, and strength.

To be a 300-game winner, a pitcher has to have no long interruptions in his career. And his career has to be lengthy. Along the way, nearly everything has to go just right. Of course, it helps to play with good teams, but that has not always been mandatory.

More than anything, though, the feat demands extraordinary skill and relentlessly good health. There is no room for mediocrity or sustained injury. To enter the charmed circle of 300-game winners, only the finest pitchers with the strongest arms need apply.

Emerging victorious in 300 or more games during a career is an accomplishment that has few parallels in baseball. No other pitching feat can match it, and among batters, only slugging 500 home runs or collecting 3,000 hits is comparable.

Given the fact that just 20 pitchers have won 300 or more games since baseball was first recognized as a major league sport in 1871—indeed, only 97 pitchers have won 200 or more games in that time—it is no wonder that these mound masters have a special place in baseball history. Nor should it come as a surprise that each one of them is a member of the Hall of Fame.

There are other similarities. Nine of the pitchers achieved their 300th win while working in the National League, and nine hurlers reached 300 as American Leaguers. One climbed to the summit while performing in the Players League and one got there as a member of the Federal League.

Seven pitchers won most of their games in the 19th century. Six reached the 300 level between 1982 and 1990. The group includes 16 righthanders and four southpaws. Sixteen of the 20 pitchers hurled complete games when they got their 300th win. Five won by one run. Phil Niekro was the only pitcher to toss a shutout. Walter Johnson was the only one to win his 300th while working in relief. Eight hurlers won their 300th game after reaching their 40th birthdays.

Ironically, the first three 300-game winners were all born on holidays. Pud Galvin entered the world on Christmas Day, Tim Keefe arrived on New Year's Day, and Mickey Welch drew his first breath on the Fourth of July.

No pitchers were subjected to greater changes in the way a ball was pitched than the early 300-game winners. Originally, the pitching mound stood 45 feet from home plate. It was moved back to 50 feet in 1880, then to 60 feet, 6 inches in 1893. The early hurlers were also required to throw with an underhand motion. Overhand deliveries were first permitted in the National League in 1884.

It should be noted that among baseball historians, as well as in various books of records, there is not unanimous agreement regarding the statistics or even the actual 300th win of some of the pitchers, particularly the early ones. Using the Baseball Hall of Fame, the Society for American Baseball Research, and *Total Baseball* as primary sources, we have attempted to clarify these discrepancies as accurately as possible.

Beyond being incredibly talented pitchers, baseball's 300-game winners are collectively a fascinating group that is readily recognized for its many other outstanding achievements. For instance, Grover Cleveland Alexander fired 16 shutouts in one season. Don Sutton never missed a turn in 23 years. Nolan Ryan tossed seven no-hitters and 12 one-hitters. And Welch completed the first 105 games he started.

Numerous other noteworthy facts accompany the pitchers' resumes. Christy Mathewson originally signed a contract with the Philadelphia Athletics. Cy Young won 20 games or more in a season 14 times in a row. Eddie Plank, Lefty Grove, and Warren Spahn didn't win their first big league games until they were 25 years old. Charles (Old Hoss) Radbourn won 60 games in a single season. Johnson once ran for Congress. Steve Carlton ran every day in a tub of rice. Kid Nichols won 30 or more games in seven different seasons. And Tom Seaver's boyhood idol was Robin Roberts.

Mentioning Roberts suggests just how hard it is to win 300 games. He didn't do it, stopping at 286. Nor did numerous other prominent Hall of Famers, such as Carl Hubbell, Herb Pennock, Bob Feller, Bob Gibson, Whitey Ford, Ted Lyons, Jim Palmer, Juan Marichal, Don Drysdale, or Ferguson Jenkins. Some Hall of Famers, including Rube Waddell, Ed Walsh, Dazzy Vance, Dizzy Dean, and Sandy Koufax, didn't even win 200 games during their careers.

In some cases, there were extenuating circumstances. Playing with bad teams, extended military service, injuries, and early retirements kept some pitchers from joining the 300-win ranks. But regardless of the reason, there is no difficulty reaching the conclusion that winning 300 games is a remarkable accomplishment that among members of the pitching fraternity has no equal.

So, this is a book about some very special pitchers who have a very special place in baseball history. It is a book that while celebrating the playing careers of these pitchers is also intended to provide information—some of it tragic—about them as people. In the process, it is hoped that *Winningest Pitchers* serves as a documentary of one of baseball's most glorious and difficult achievements.

Winningest Pitchers

Pud Galvin

The First 300-Game Winner

The first major league pitcher to win 300 games was a short, stocky, easy-going righthander who was a notoriously tireless worker and owner of a ferocious fastball that turned everyday hitters into quivering weaklings.

Standing just 5 feet, 8 inches and usually weighing at least 190 pounds, Jim (Pud) Galvin bore little resemblance to the sleek hurlers who populated most pitching mounds. But give him the ball, and mere physical appearance suddenly became as unimportant as last week's newspapers.

With a ball in his grasp, the underhand-throwing Galvin, who pitched from 45- then 50-foot distances between home plate and the pitchers mound, was a terror. Not only was he the possessor of an intimidating fastball, but he had a changeup that drove batters crazy. Galvin didn't throw a curve. He didn't consider it necessary.

The evidence suggests that he was right. Although he never pitched for a club that finished above third place, Galvin won 361

Through most of his career, **Pud Galvin** pitched every other day.

games during his 14-year career. Twice in succession he won 46 games in a single season, he won 20 or more 10 different times, and he is the owner of two no-hitters.

Pud, who got that nickname because it was said that he made pudding out of opposing batters, had the ultimate work ethic. Most of the time, he pitched every other day. He worked more innings (5,941) and completed more games (639) than any hurler in baseball history except Cy Young. Galvin worked in more than 300 innings in 10 different seasons. He also ranks second in most losses (308).

Overall, Galvin, also called "Gentle Jeems" because of his easy-going nature, and "The Little Steam Engine" for his relentless work habits, pitched in 697 major league games. He started 681 of them, with 57 being shutouts. He struck out 1,799 and walked 744, which over the length of his career comes to about one base on balls every eight innings. Pud had a career 2.87 ERA.

Not only did Galvin have outstanding control, he was a master at picking off base-runners. Once he walked the first three batters in a game. He then picked off each one.

"If I ever had Galvin to catch, no one would ever steal a base on me," said Hall of Fame catcher Buck Ewing of the New York Giants. "That fellow keeps them glued to the bag. You notice that funny, false motion of his that can't really be called a balk. He fooled me so badly one day that I never even attempted to get back to first base. And he certainly also has the best control of any pitcher in this league."

Sometimes, when he wasn't pitching, Galvin played in the field. Although not an accomplished hitter—his career batting average was just .202—he appeared in 51 games as an outfielder, plus two as a shortstop. Also regarded as a splendid fielder, he had his best year with the bat in 1886 when he hit .253 in 194 at-bats. In 1887, he hit a home run in Pittsburgh that they talked about for years. The eighth-inning blast sailed over the center field fence and gave the Alleghenys a 1–0 win over Boston.

It took an excessively long time for the modern world to note Galvin's accomplishments, but the pudgy hurler was finally voted into the Hall of Fame in 1965 by the Veterans Committee. When he was inducted, writer/historian Lee Allen said, "It is difficult to recall when a player elected to membership in the Hall of Fame brought with him more robust qualifications than Galvin." Added Lefty Grove, "My numbers appear insignificant compared to his."

Galvin's induction occurred 63 years after he had died penniless in a shabby rooming house in Pittsburgh. Pud's passing went almost unnoticed as flood waters from the Ohio River ravaged a nearby neighborhood, leaving thousands homeless. Suffering from pneumonia, Galvin had been confined to a bed for nearly three months when he died in 1902 of what was reported as "catarrh of the stomach." Accounts of the day said he had been unconscious for five days. Broke from an ill-advised business venture, Galvin, 45, left no money to pay for his funeral. Friends from in and out of baseball raised the necessary funds to pay for the burial and to help Galvin's wife and the couple's six (out of 11 originally) surviving children.

Life had started out on a much happier note for Galvin. Born on Christmas Day in 1856 in an Irish neighborhood in St. Louis known as Kerry Patch, a baseball hotbed, Galvin began playing baseball at an early age. By his late teens, he had become the top amateur player in St. Louis.

Galvin had trained as a steamfitter but found baseball much more appealing. And in 1875 at the tender age of 18, he signed with the St. Louis Brown Stockings, a member of the National Association, the first recognized major league. Galvin was uneducated and largely unrefined. As a teenager, according to baseball historian Joseph Overfield, he wore only flannel shirts and ate with his fingers. Appalled by his untidy habits, other players made him eat in the hotel kitchen.

Galvin, who later switched to wearing white duck pants, patent leather shoes, and a straw hat, posted a 4–2 record in eight games. After the season, however, the five-year-old National Association disbanded. Pud hooked up with the St. Louis Red Stockings, an independent professional team, and in 1876 won 31 of 47 decisions, including a no-hitter against Philadelphia and a perfect game against the prominent Cass Club of Detroit.

The following year the fireballing righthander joined Allegheny, a member of the International Association, the first minor league and Pittsburgh's first professional club.

At one point, Galvin pitched four shutouts in 19 days while winning 12 and losing six.

In 1878, Galvin jumped to the Buffalo Bisons of the same IA and went 28–10. The next season, when Buffalo joined the National League, Galvin made his big league debut with a sizzling 37–27 record. Over a two-year period, he pitched in 106 of the Bisons' 116 games, completing 96 of them. At one point, the Bisons played 22 games, and Galvin started and completed each one of them.

One newspaper account of the day could hardy contain itself about Galvin's mound exploits. "In Galvin, Buffalo has the speediest pitcher in his profession," gushed the Syracuse *Courier*. "The celebrity of his pitches is a marvel to behold and it is a wonder he can find the catchers to hold him."

Galvin, who sported a wide, flowing handlebar mustache, stayed with Buffalo until 1885—with the exception of a short stint when, after getting involved in a contract dispute, he jumped to the California League in 1880. He left California, despite having signed a contract, and while departing had to hike 36 miles to escape a group of armed local police who were attempting to thwart his getaway.

Back in Buffalo, he was greeted as a returning hero. "The picturesque form of the mild-mannered pitcher was recognized by loud, continuous applause," said the Buffalo *Express*. "A smile illuminated his classic countenance and he bowed modestly."

Pud was rapidly becoming one of the most highly acclaimed pitchers in the National League. After winning 20 in 1880, he went 28–24 and 28–23 before exploding to 46–29 and 46–22 seasons in 1883 and 1884.

In 1880, Galvin pitched his first major league no-hitter, blanking the Worcester Brown Stockings, 1–0. He registered his second no-hitter in 1884 with an 18–0 decision over the Detroit Wolverines. The no-hitters made Galvin only the second major league pitcher (after Larry Corcoran) to record two no-hitters in a career.

In that era, Galvin had many other outstanding achievements. In 1882, he beat Worcester in both ends of a doubleheader, 9–5 and 18–8. In 1884 against Detroit, he pitched a one-hitter, the no-hitter, and a three-hitter just six days apart, then the eighth day lost 1–0 in 12 innings. During that span, he pitched 38 consecutive scoreless innings and allowed 12 hits and one run (unearned) while striking out 36 and walking none. Galvin also ended the 18-game winning streak of Old Hoss Radbourn, who won 60 that year, and the 20-game winning streak of the Providence Grays when he notched a 2–0 victory in 1884.

The 1883 and 1884 seasons were by far Galvin's best. In 1883, he worked in 76 games and 656 innings, completing 72 of the 75 games he started. The next season, he appeared in 636 innings, completing 71 of the 72 games in which he appeared and firing 12 shutouts. He struck out 369, one of the highest totals of the 19th century, while walking just 63.

While playing in Buffalo, Galvin also became friendly with the local sheriff. Eventually, the sheriff, Grover Cleveland, became mayor of the city and, still later, President of the United States. The two remained close friends long after their careers went separate ways. Once, when a team of baseball players visited the White House, Cleveland asked, "How's my old friend Jimmy Galvin?"

Galvin was named manager of the Buffalo team for the 1885 season, but after winning just seven of 24 games, he was relieved of his duties. Soon afterward, although he had won 218 games for Buffalo, the Bisons sold Galvin to the Pittsburgh Alleghenys of the American Association for a reported $2,500, an almost unheard of figure at that time. Galvin was given $700 of the purchase price and a lofty $3,000 contract, representing a raise of some $1,000 and making him at the time baseball's highest-paid player.

Although modest and unassuming and a man with legions of friends, Pud was never shy about making financial demands, especially when he switched teams. "They talk about slaves," he said. "Every time they sold me, I benefited by the operation."

Galvin would not leave Pittsburgh until 1892. He registered a 29–21 mark in 1886, and when the club joined the National

League the following year, he went 28–21. Galvin won for the franchise that would eventually be called the Pirates the team's first two games in its new circuit, beating John Clarkson and the Chicago White Stockings, 6–2, and Lady Baldwin and Detroit, 8–5.

In 1888, Galvin became the first major league pitcher to win 300 games. He reached the charmed circle October 5, 1888, beating the Washington Nationals with a four-hitter, 5–1. There were 14 errors in the game, including nine by the losers, and only one earned run.

That season and the next, he won 23 games each year, then in 1890 became one of many players to jump to the newly formed Players or Brotherhood League. The National League was said to have offered Pud $8,000 and a house to come back, but he rejected the offer out of loyalty to his fellow Brotherhood players. Remaining in Pittsburgh and playing with the Burghers, Pud won just 12 of 25 decisions in the circuit's only season. About the most noteworthy occurrence during the season came when Galvin faced Tim Keefe in the first battle of 300-game winners. Pud won that confrontation, 8–2. He and Keefe would square off three more times (with Galvin winning once) in what would be the last meeting of 300-game winners until Phil Niekro and Don Sutton tangled in 1986.

Galvin returned in 1891 to the newly named Pirates, whose catcher was a slender young stalwart named Connie Mack. Pud's career was obviously on the decline. Realizing that, the Pirates acquired veteran hurlers Mark (Fido) Baldwin and Silver King in 1891. Galvin was pushed to the background and his salary was cut in half. Midway through the 1892 season, after Galvin had won 24 games in one and one-half seasons with the Pirates, he was sold to the St. Louis Browns. Hurting from a leg injury suffered from a collision with Cap Anson, Pud finished an uneventful season in his hometown.

The following year he tried to stay in baseball as a National League umpire but did not deal well with the arguments and abuse and quit after just one season. Galvin attempted a comeback in 1894 as a pitcher with Buffalo, now a member of the Eastern League, but that did not work out either.

Returning to Pittsburgh, Galvin tried his hand at different jobs, working as a bartender and in construction. Eventually, he opened his own saloon, which was billed as the largest in Pittsburgh. Pud employed nine bartenders, but while each of them was said to have later opened his own bar, Galvin, a poor business-man, soon went broke and was forced to close the business.

Having saved little of the substantial money he had earned as a player and by now weighing well over 300 pounds, Galvin sank rapidly into a financial abyss from which he wouldn't recover. Forced into a meager existence, he died a pauper, a tragic contrast to the glamorous life he once led.

October 5, 1888—Alleghenys 5, Nationals 1

Pittsburgh	AB	R	H	Washington	AB	R	H
Miller, c	4	1	0	Hoy, cf	4	0	1
McShannic, 3b	4	0	0	Myers, 2b	4	0	1
Smith, 2b	4	0	0	Wilmot, lf	4	0	0
Coleman, 1b	4	1	1	O'Brien, 1b	4	0	0
Kuehne, ss	4	0	1	Mack, c	4	1	0
Fields, lf	4	2	1	Dailey, rf	3	0	0
Maul, rf	4	0	1	Donnelly, 3b	4	0	1
Nichols, cf	3	1	0	Shoch, ss	3	0	0
Galvin, p	4	0	0	Haddock, p	3	0	1
Totals	35	5	4		33	1	4

Pittsburgh	0	2	0	0	0	0	0	2	1	–	5
Washington	0	1	0	0	0	0	0	0	0	–	1

Pittsburgh	IP	H	R	ER	BB	SO
Galvin (W)	9	4	1	0	0	1
Washington						
Haddock (L)	9	4	5	1	1	0

DP–Pittsburgh 2. E–McShannick 2, Smith 3, Myers 2, Wilmot 1, O'Brien 1, Donnelly 1, Shoch 3, Haddock 1. 3B–Fields. SB–Coleman, Kuehne, Fields, Maul. T–1:30.

Tim Keefe

Strong Will Prevails

It is obvious that Tim Keefe grew up to be one of the first prominent major league pitchers despite his early surroundings. That speaks volumes for the determination of the second big league hurler to become a 300-game winner.

Unlike some other children with athletic ability, Keefe was not encouraged to pursue a career in baseball. Just the opposite, young Tim was frequently beaten by his father when he was caught out in the back lot trying to perfect his natural talent.

Born New Year's Day, 1857, Keefe grew up in Cambridge, Massachusetts. His father, Patrick, a native of Ireland, built factories for a living, a job that often sent him on out-of-town assignments. Unfortunately for Patrick, when the Civil War broke out, he was in the wrong place at the wrong time.

Helping to construct a factory below the Mason-Dixon line, Patrick was sent to a Confederate jail when he refused to join the rebel

Tim Keefe was the first major league pitcher to strike out 2,000 batters.

army. He spent three years in the prison, making bullets. Meanwhile, two of his brothers were killed fighting with the Union army.

When the somewhat scarred Patrick finally returned to Cambridge, he discovered that his nine-year-old son Tim had developed a special fondness for baseball. Insisting that the boy spend his time learning mathematics instead of wasting it on something as useless as baseball, Patrick gave his son a sound thrashing whenever he caught him with a ball or bat in his hands.

Patrick, however, underestimated his son's willpower. Determined to be a baseball player, Tim continued to play despite his father's abusive treatment. Eventually, the youngster's resolve was rewarded.

Some years later, Keefe not only became just the second big league pitcher to win 300 games; he also became the first major leaguer to strike out 2,000 batters. Twice he won more than 40 games in a season. He set a record with 19 straight wins. And he became one of the first hurlers to perfect the art of throwing a change of pace.

Keefe's career was, to say the least, unusual. He played in three different major leagues, which allowed him to perform in some 47 different ballparks, by far more than anyone else has ever done. He was one of the driving forces behind the formation of the Players League. And he was one of the few pitchers who experienced drastic changes in the pitchers' mound when during his career the distance from the mound to home plate was lengthened from 45 feet to 50 feet and finally to 60 feet, 6 inches.

A sidearm thrower, Keefe spent 14 years at the top rung of the baseball ladder. Over that span, he compiled a 342–225 record with a 2.62 earned run average. Of the 600 games in which he worked, the 5-foot, 10½-inch, 185-pounder started 594 of them, completing 554, the third highest total in big league history. In 5,047 innings, Keefe allowed 4,432 hits, struck out 2,560, and walked 1,236. He hurled 39 shutouts.

Keefe, who was often called Sir Timothy because of his serious, quiet, and gentlemanly demeanor, led his league in ERA three times, and in various other categories including wins, complete games, strikeouts, and innings pitched, each twice. A smart pitcher who relied on control and location, he was equipped with a good fastball and curve, but early in his career he added a change-up to his offerings after becoming one of the first hurlers to perfect the pitch.

Never one to rest on his laurels, Keefe constantly explored ways to improve himself, both on and off the field. In *Kings of the Diamond*, authors Lee Allen and Tom Meany relate how there was a time early in his career when Keefe would disappear after a game, never to be seen for the rest of the evening by his teammates. Finally, it was discovered that Tim was holing up in his hotel room each night, teaching himself shorthand. It was a skill he thought he could use if his baseball career was suddenly terminated.

Fortunately for him, Keefe never had to test his knowledge of shorthand. Instead of making symbols on paper, he spent the best part of his life making enemy bats work like paper. And in acknowledgement of his special achievements, Tim was inducted into the Hall of Fame in 1964 after being selected by the Veterans Committee.

That was 31 years after his death of a heart attack at the age of 76 and 71 years after he'd fired his final pitch following a major league career that had taken him from Troy to New York to Philadelphia.

Keefe had escaped his father's wrath and begun playing on amateur baseball teams as a teenager in the mid-1870s. First, he played on Cambridge teams, then branched out, joining clubs in Boston and ultimately in other parts of New England. Eventually, he made the jump to the professional level, signing with Utica, a minor league. He then pitched for teams in the same minor league at New Bedford and Albany before getting the call to the big leagues late in the 1880 season with Troy.

In his first National League appearance, Keefe, pitching from a mound that was in its last year of measuring 45 feet from home plate, fired a four-hitter while leading Troy to a 4–2 victory over the Cincinnati Reds. Although he appeared in just 12 games with the Haymakers (posting a 6–6 record), Keefe ended the season with a sparkling 0.86 ERA. Tim was on his way.

Two more years playing for a downtrodden Troy team resulted in a combined 35–53 record for Keefe, who tossed a one-hitter and two two-hitters while being paired with Mickey Welch as the club's main pitchers.

Welch was impressed by the way Keefe operated. "I never saw a better pitcher," he said many years later. "True, he did his best work at 50 feet, but he still would have had no superior at 60 feet, 6 inches. He was also one of the finest gentlemen I ever played ball with."

But while the two young hurlers were on the way up, Troy was on the way out. The franchise folded after the 1882 season and was relocated to New York, where it became that city's first National League baseball team.

Keefe, who pitched five one-hitters during his career, went to New York, too, but as a member of the Metropolitans of the American Association. That team was also in its first year of existence in the two-year-old AA. Curiously, it was owned by John Day, who also owned New York's new National League club.

As one of the original Mets, Keefe's career flourished. With the mound having been moved back several years earlier to 50 feet, Keefe had no trouble switching teams, and in his first year he logged in at 41–27 in what would be one of his finest years. During the season, Tim had one of the most noteworthy days in pitching history when, on July 4, he won both games of a doubleheader over the Columbus Buckeyes, firing a one-hitter in the morning contest and a two-hitter in the afternoon. No pitcher hurling both ends of a doubleheader ever allowed fewer combined hits.

Keefe tossed another one-hitter against Louisville later in the season. He finished the campaign with a 2.41 ERA but, more significantly, worked in a career-high 619 innings while completing each of the 68 games he started and leading the league with 359 strikeouts, also a career high.

A master strategist when he toed the rubber, Keefe was almost as good the following year when his 37–17 record helped the Mets to New York's first pennant as manager Jim Mutrie's club finished six and one-half games ahead of Columbus in the 13-team American Association. In baseball's first version of a "world series," the Mets met the Providence Grays, the National League champs, in what turned out to be a three-game set at the Polo Grounds.

Tim lost the first two games, 6–0 and 3–1 to Old Hoss Radbourn, as the Mets were swept in three games.

In 1885, Keefe was reunited with his old pitching mate Mickey Welch after Day decided to transfer Tim, manager Mutrie, and one other player to his National League club's roster. Although arm trouble kept Keefe out of action in the early weeks of the season, he bounced back to finish the year with a 32–13 record while leading the league with a spectacular 1.58 ERA.

Keefe had another fine season in 1886 when he posted a 42–20 record while completing 62 of the 64 games he started and working in a league-leading 535 innings. In 1887, Tim suffered what was described as a "nervous breakdown" after an errant fastball of his hit an opposing batter in the head. But he came back to finish the season with a 35–19 record.

Tim continued to baffle enemy batsmen in 1888, especially when he set a new record for one season with 19 consecutive wins during a seven-week period extending from June 23 until August 10. The record has never been surpassed, although it was tied in 1912 by the Giants' Rube Marquard. (Some historians have questioned the validity of Keefe's streak because in one game against Chicago he was relieved with the Giants leading 9–0 after two innings. But because the rules of the day gave Keefe the victory, his streak has been left intact.)

Keefe ended the season with a 35–12 record, making six straight years of 30 or more wins. He also struck out 335, giving him his third 300-plus strikeout season (a feat that stood until Nolan Ryan came along). And the Giants walked off with their first pennant, outdistancing Cap Anson's Chicago White Stockings by nine games. In a 10-game post-season "world series" against the St. Louis Browns, Keefe captured four of the Giants' six wins, triumphing in the opener on a three-hitter, 2–1, the third game, 4–2, the fifth game, 6–4, and the eighth game, 11–3.

After a prolonged holdout the following year, Keefe eventually wrangled a $4,500 contract, which made him one of the highest-paid players of the 19th century. Eventually, taking the mound in late April, Keefe went on to a 28–13 record, and the Giants again won the pennant, edging the Boston Beaneaters by one game. This time, in the post-season playoffs, New York defeated the Brooklyn Bridegrooms, six games to three, but Keefe pitched in only two games, with a 12–10 loss in the opener being his only decision.

Keefe had other worlds to conquer, however. Major league players were unhappy with their low salaries and the absence of other rights, and in 1890 a full-scale revolt was underway. Keefe was one of the leaders.

Tim and more than 100 other players left the National League and formed an eight-team Players (or Brotherhood) League. Pitching for his third New York team—this one was also called the Giants—Keefe went 17–11 during a season that, according to John J. O'Malley in the Society for American Baseball Research's *Baseball's First Stars,* was cut short in early September when Tim broke the index finger of his pitching hand during a practice session. Earlier in the season, Keefe had won 10 straight games.

One of those victories was a 9–4 decision over the Boston Reds on June 4, giving Tim the 300th victory of his big league career. In that game, played on a terribly hot day in New York, Keefe surrendered eight hits while striking out seven and walking three. Fortunately for Keefe, his pitching arm was working because his fielding sure wasn't. Tim made four errors on a day when the teams combined for 14 bobbles. There were only four earned runs in the game.

The Players League folded after one season, and Keefe returned in 1891 to the National League Giants.

He didn't stay long in New York. After appearing in eight games, Tim was dealt to the Philadelphia Phillies. He finished the season with a combined 5–11 record in 19 games.

Keefe was the Phillies opening day pitcher in 1892, losing to Amos Rusie and the New York Giants, 5–4. Later in the season, he beat the St. Louis Browns (now in the National League) and Pud Galvin, 2–0, in a battle of 300-game winners. Tim finished the season with a 19–16 mark. Then in 1893, with the pitching mound set back to 60 feet, 6 inches, he closed out his career with a 10–7 record.

It was not easy to get baseball out of his system, however, so Keefe applied for a job as a National League umpire. He worked three years in that capacity, but the constant battles with players made the man who never questioned an umpire's decision uncomfortable. Finally, after one particularly acrimonious game in 1896, during which he made several hotly disputed calls and was reviled by players and fans and needed a police escort to get him safely off the field, Keefe quit.

Tim returned to Cambridge, where he opened and ran for many years thereafter a real estate business. He also coached baseball at Harvard, Princeton, and Tufts.

June 4, 1890—Giants 9, Reds 4

Boston	AB	R	H	New York	AB	R	H
Brown, cf	5	0	1	Gore, cf	4	3	3
H. Richardson, lf	5	0	1	Ewing, c	4	3	2
Stovey, rf	4	1	1	Connor, 1b	3	0	1
Nash, 3b	3	1	0	O'Rourke, rf	5	0	1
Brouthers, 1b	3	0	0	D. Richardson, 2b	4	1	1
Murphy, c	4	1	1	Slattery, lf	5	0	2
Irwin, ss	3	1	1	Shannon, ss	5	1	2
Quinn, 2b	4	0	2	Hatfield, 3b	5	1	2
Madden, p	1	0	0	Keefe, p	5	0	0
Gumbert, p	3	0	1				
Totals	35	4	8		40	9	14

| **Boston** | 0 0 0 0 1 3 0 0 0 – 4 |
| **New York** | 3 0 1 0 1 3 0 1 x – 9 |

DP–Boston. E–Brouthers, Murphy 2, Irwin, Madden 2, Gumbert 3, Shannon 1, Keefe 4. 2B–Gore 2, Shannon, Hatfield, Irwin. 3B–Shannon, Gumbert. SB–Stovey, Shannon, D. Richardson. Earned Runs–Boston 1, New York 3. Base on Balls–Madden 2, Gumbert 3, Keefe 3. Strikeouts–Madden 1, Gumbert 1, Keefe 7. WP–Keefe. T–2:05.

Mickey Welch

A Lot to Smile About

It is not a common trait of pitchers to possess a good sense of humor. For the most part, the job does not lend itself to wit and whimsey.

But there have been some notable exceptions. One of them was Mickey Welch, a diminutive righthander who, while toiling in the major leagues for 13 seasons, became baseball's third 300-game winner.

Welch's nickname was "Smiling Mickey." And in a game in which no rule says that a pitcher has to be serious all of the time, he easily lived up to his billing.

As his nickname suggests, the easy-going Welch usually had a smile on his face. An extremely friendly and likeable chap, Mickey almost always had a cheerful word for everyone he met, including fans. He also wasn't opposed to a good joke or a comical retort.

Welch, a noted clean-liver who neither drank, smoked, nor swore and who never wore a moustache or sideburns even though

One season, **Mickey Welch** tossed three complete game wins in two days.

they were fashionable at the time, was once asked the secret of his success. "Drink a lot of beer," he joked.

At the peak of his career, Smiling Mickey, a name said to have been given to him by a popular cartoonist of the day, earned $4,000, a glorious sum for a pre-20th-century player. "Believe me, I worked for it," he said.

And so he did. Six times during his career, Welch worked in more than 400 innings. He completed the first 105 games in which he pitched. Once he hurled three complete game victories in two days.

The 5-foot, 8-inch, 160-pound Welch was a workhorse, all right. He appeared on the mound in 4,802 innings. He worked in 564 games and completed 525 of the 549 he started. Four times he had more than 50 complete games in a season, once completing all 64 of his starts. He has the sixth highest total of complete games in baseball history.

When he wasn't pitching, Welch sometimes played in center field. He performed in 59 games as an outfielder, while carrying a lifetime batting average of .224 with 13 home runs. Some historians claim that Mickey was the first pinch-hitter ever used in a major league game when he batted for Hank O'Day in 1889.

Mickey's big league career began in Troy and ended in New York. Along the way, he registered a 307–210 record with an earned run average of 2.71. Only three other pitchers in baseball gave up more runs than Welch's 2,556. He yielded 4,588 hits while striking out 1,850. With control that was less than pinpoint, he walked 1,297, three times leading the National League in bases on balls. Mickey ranks third on the all-time list in wild pitches with 274.

Never a hard thrower, Welch relied on a variety of curves and an early version of the screwball. "He was a cunning little fellow," one writer of the day declared, "rather than a speedy one."

"I had to use my head," Welch said in a quote uncovered by Irv Bergman in the Society for American Baseball Research's *Baseball's First Stars.* "I studied the hitters and I knew how to pitch to all of them. I had a pretty good fastball, but I depended chiefly on a change of pace and an assortment of curve balls."

There was no question about the effectiveness of the elfin hurler's deliveries. He became just the third pitcher to win 300 games when he reached that magic level in 1892 while engaged with the New York Giants.

Welch was elected to the Hall of Fame in 1973, a selection put forth by the Veterans Committee. It was a fitting tribute to a moundsman who had won as many as 44 games in a single season, who once won 17 games in a row, who tossed 40 career shutouts, winning 10 of them by 1–0 scores, and who got the win in the first game ever played at the original Polo Grounds in New York.

The path to the major leagues and eventual fame and glory was a rather direct one for Mickey. Born on the Fourth of July in 1859 in Brooklyn, New York, he learned the game on local sandlots before embarking on a baseball career at the age of 18.

The young pitcher's first paying job was in 1877 with the Poughkeepsie (New York) Volunteers, an independent team. While earning $45 a month, Welch won 16 of 22 games.

Mickey became a full-fledged professional the following year when he joined a team in Auburn, New York. Later that season, he switched to a club in Holyoke, Massachusetts. After a 23–14 record there in 1879, he was summoned to the big leagues with Troy, then a member of the National League.

In 1880, Troy was hardly one of the pillars of the five-year-old circuit. But, managed by Bob (Death to Flying Things) Ferguson, the New York club did have one notable distinction. The Haymakers (or Trojans, as they were sometimes called) had four rookies who would eventually find their ways to the Hall of Fame. Along with Welch, they were pitcher Tim Keefe, catcher William (Buck) Ewing, and infielder Roger Connor.

Keefe and Welch not only formed the backbone of Troy's pitching staff, but they would become the first great mound duo in baseball history. Mickey's star emerged first when he went 34–30 in his rookie season, working 574 innings and completing all 64 of the games he started in what was the final year of the 45-foot distance between the pitching mound and home plate. He also hit .287 that season while playing two games in the outfield.

With the move to a 50-foot gap between pitcher and batter, Welch's production dropped off in 1881 when he managed a mere 21–18 record for a second-division Troy team. But he completed 40 of his 40 starts to keep his streak alive.

Welch slipped to 14–16 in 1882, but Troy tumbled even farther. The Haymakers fell clean out of the National League, one of two teams (the other was the Worcester Brown Stockings) that disbanded. The Troy franchise was reborn in New York as the Gothams (Worcester became the Philadelphia Phillies).

The Gothams' home field, located near Central Park, was the first of several ballparks that would be called the Polo Grounds. In the first game there, with a huge crowd including President Ulysses S. Grant on hand, Welch hurled his team to victory. It would be the first of 25 wins (against 23 losses) logged by Mickey during a season in which his 105 straight complete-game winning streak would come to a close. He also played in 38 games in the outfield that year.

As unhappy as he was that the streak had ended, Mickey was even more disturbed by the fact that he was only pitching every other day. He thought he should climb the hill more often than that, and in an attempt to remedy the situation, he became one of baseball's earliest contract negotiators. Welch insisted that the team add a clause in his contract that said he could pitch more frequently than every other day. The Gothams complied, and for the rest of his career, the clause appeared in all of Mickey's contracts.

At best, the Gothams were also-rans in the National League in their early years, but there was nothing mediocre about Welch. Getting more starts, he posted a 39–21 record in 1884 while finishing 62 of his 65 starts and toiling in 557 innings. He also registered 345 strikeouts, by far the highest total of his career. In an August 28 game against the Cleveland Blues, Mickey set a major league record by fanning the first nine batters he faced.

If he wasn't already regarded as one of the premier twirlers in baseball, Welch certified that rating in 1885. Starting with a one-hitter on opening day over the Boston Beaneaters, Mickey had his best year, going 44–11 with a career-low 1.66 ERA. His .800 winning percentage led the National League (the only time he led the league in any category except walks), and he completed each of the 55 games he started while appearing in 492 innings.

In a two-day period, he gave a classic demonstration of his durability. Mickey beat the Chicago White Stockings, 1–0, in 10 innings at New York. That night the team took a train to Buffalo, where the next day it would meet the Bisons in a July 4 doubleheader. Celebrating his birthday, Welch won the morning game, 6–0, then came back to win in the afternoon, 6–2, giving him three victories and 28 innings pitched in only a little more than 24 hours.

At one point in 1885, Welch won 17 straight games, four of them being shutouts and four of them being games in which he allowed just one run. Mickey beat Buffalo, 24–0, in the most one-sided game of the season in a mismatch during which the little hurler scored five runs and allowed five hits.

The 1885 season was noteworthy in New York for two other reasons. The name of the team was switched to Giants after manager Jim Mutrie in a particular moment of ecstasy following a victory had bellowed, "My big fellows, my giants." And Keefe had joined the team after spending two years with the American Association New York Metropolitans.

In their first year of being reunited, Welch and Keefe (32–13) combined for 76 of the Giants' 85 wins.

The brilliant duo captured all 75 of the Giants' wins in 1886, with Welch going 33–22 while working in 500 innings but leading the league in walks for the third year in a row. Mickey went 22–15 the following year, then recorded marks of 26–19 and 27–12 over the next two seasons.

With Welch and Keefe combining for 61 victories, the Giants won their first National League pennant in 1888. That fall, in a forerunner of the World Series, New York met the American Association's St. Louis Browns. The Giants won six of the 10 games played, with Welch losing the second game, 3–0, and winning the sixth outing—curiously played in Philadelphia—12–5, getting the nod over Elton Chamberlain each time.

The Giants returned to the post-season playoffs in 1889 after Welch and Keefe totaled 55 wins together. This time, facing the AA's Brooklyn Bridegrooms, the Giants won six of nine games. Welch, pitching only once, however, was an 8–7 loser in the third game.

Out of loyalty to the Giants, Mickey resisted the overtures of the Players League in 1890, but by then his career was winding down. He posted a 17–14 record, his lowest victory total since 1882. Welch did, however, win his 300th game that season, beating Pittsburgh, then called the Infants, 4–2, on July 28. "Welch's curves were too much for the local men," a Pittsburgh newspaper reported. With just 147 fans watching, Mickey gave up five hits. He struck out three and walked two. He also made three errors

His arm, finally showing the strains of years of hard work, Welch stumbled to a 5–9 record in 1891 while taking the mound just 22 times. He appeared in only one game for New York in 1892 before getting sent down to—of all places—Troy, by then a Giants farm club. Welsh logged a 17–14 record in 31 games at Troy, then retired at the end of the season.

Soon thereafter, Mickey moved to Holyoke, where he served for a number of years as steward of the Elks Club. He returned in 1912 to New York when John McGraw offered him a job as a gatekeeper at the bleacher entrance of the Polo Grounds. Mickey was still working that job into the 1940s, entertaining fans with his stories about the "old days" and, of course, charming them with his infectious smile.

Smiling Mickey, a man who enjoyed life to the fullest, died in 1941 at the age of 82 while visiting a grandson in Concord, New Hampshire.

July 28, 1890—Giants 4, Infants 2

New York	AB	R	H	Pittsburgh	AB	R	H
Tiernan, cf	3	1	2	Decker, c	4	0	1
Hornung, 1b	4	0	0	Miller, 3b	3	1	1
Bassett, 2b	4	0	0	Laroque, 2b	4	0	0
Burkett, cf	3	1	1	Hecker, 1b	4	1	1
Glasscock, ss	4	1	2	Berger, rf	4	0	1
Denny, 3b	4	1	3	Osborne, lf	4	0	0
Henry, lf	3	0	1	Sales, ss	3	0	1
Clark, c	3	0	1	Wilson, cf	2	0	0
Welch, p	3	0	0	Baker, p	2	0	0
Totals	31	4	10		30	2	5

```
New York     1 0 0 0 0 3 0 0 0  -  4
Pittsburgh   2 0 0 0 0 0 0 0 0  -  2
```

New York	IP	H	R	ER	BB	SO
Welch (W)	9	5	2	2	2	3

Pittsburgh						
Baker (L)	9	10	4	2	2	1

DP–Pittsburgh. E–Hornung, Welch 3, Decker, Baker 2. 2B–Hecker. 3B–Tiernan. SB–Miller. PB–Decker. HBP–Wilson (by Welch). T–2:00. A–147.

Old Hoss Radbourn

Never Too Tired to Pitch

Before there were cars and airplanes, before there were radios, televisions, telephones, and even indoor plumbing, Charles (Old Hoss) Radbourn had a curve ball. He threw it with dazzling effectiveness at a time when few others had any inkling that the pitch existed, much less knew how to throw it.

Radbourn also had a hopping fastball, a fadeaway, and a bewildering changeup. Although he made all of his deliveries from an underhand motion, his tosses far exceeded the capabilities of opposing hitters, and they made the strong-armed righthander the premier pitcher of the 19th century.

Clark Griffith, a fine major league pitcher before he became a team owner, said that Radbourn "had the best slow curve I ever saw. It would come up slowly and then suddenly dart downward with what looked like second-wind speed."

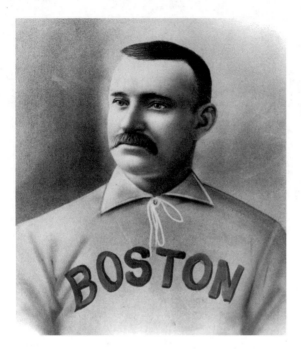

In 1884, **Old Hoss Radbourn** became baseball's only 60-game winner.

Radbourn also had superb control. Throughout his career, he averaged one walk every five innings. "Any delivery without control is no delivery at all," he said.

As good as he was, though, perhaps the most remarkable quality that set Radbourn apart from his peers was his amazing stamina. Old Hoss didn't know the meaning of an off day, a trait that not only took a heavy toll on his arm, but that also earned him his nickname.

Radbourn was not opposed to pitching nearly every day. In 1883 while pitching for the Providence Grays, he started 68 of his team's 98 games (while working in eight other games in relief). In the second half of the following year, he hurled in 41 of the Grays' final 51 games, including each of the last 22 games. And when he wasn't pitching, Radbourn often played either second base, shortstop, first base, or the outfield.

Old Hoss worked in more than 600 innings in two different seasons. Sometimes after a game his arm was so sore he couldn't raise his hand to comb his hair. Before his next start, he would have to apply hot towels to his aching arm and shoulder for several hours. He could toss a ball only a few feet as he began warming up. Eventually, he'd move back a couple of steps at a time until he reached the regulation pitching distance, which then stood at 50 feet.

"There is not a pitcher in history who went in day after day as Radbourn did, and in successive games baffled batters who never seemed able to get the hang of a delivery that was based on common sense and complete knowledge," said John Foster, writing in 1925 about the 50th anniversary of the National League.

Radbourn's most memorable achievement came in 1884 when he won 60 games for Providence, the highest total ever attained by a major league pitcher. (Some baseball historians have questioned Radbourn's 60 wins, claiming he was credited with one too many.) That year, he completed all 73 games he started while striking out 441 in 678 innings. His earned run average that year was 1.38. His salary was $3,000.

Because of the huge burden Radbourn's tireless efforts placed on his arm, his career was relatively short. He played in only 11 big league seasons. Yet he compiled a 309–195 record and a 2.67 ERA. Pitching in 528 games, Old Hoss worked 4,535 innings, yielding 4,335 hits, striking out 1,830, and walking 875. Of the 503 games he started, he completed 489 of them, a figure that ranks seventh best in baseball history.

The 5-foot, 9-inch, 165-pound hurler, whose brother George (Dordy) pitched in three games in the big leagues in 1883, had nine seasons in which he won 20 or more games. He also fired a no-hitter, blanking Cleveland, 8–0, in 1883, and seven one-hitters. At the plate, Radbourn had a career batting average of .235 with 585 hits (nine home runs) in 2,487 at-bats.

Although born December 11, 1854, in Rochester, New York, Radbourn (whose name for many years was mistakenly spelled with an *e* on the end) grew up in Bloomington, Illinois, the son of English immigrant parents. Charley's father was a butcher, an occupation that the future ballplayer tried briefly but quickly rejected as a lifetime venture.

Years later, author Roger Kahn, in his marvelous book on pitching called *The Head Game*, uncovered a report from the New York *Clipper* in which Radbourn was asked if he was tired from his excessive trips to the mound. "Tired out tossing a little five-ounce baseball for two hours?" Radbourn asked incredulously. "I used to be a butcher. From four in the morning until eight at night I knocked down steers with a 25-pound sledge. Tired from playing two hours a day for 10 times the money I used to get for 16 hours a day?"

From being a butcher in a slaughterhouse, Radbourn, who had also given higher education a brief fling with a stint at Illinois Wesleyan College, moved to the railroad business, where he became a brakeman. That had little appeal, too, to the free-spirited youngster, who according to Kahn was a "hellraiser" who drank heavily, caroused with relentless diligence, and hung around with a young baseball fan who went by the name of Jesse James.

Charley, long a baseball devotee himself, played on local town teams before hooking up at the age of 23 with a fast-paced traveling team called the Peoria Reds. The Reds faced anybody and everybody. Radbourn played mostly right field, where he hit .299 in 28 games. Although only a backup pitcher, he was good enough to attract the attention of a man named Ted Sullivan, who was in the process of putting together a new minor circuit to be known as the Northwest League.

Sullivan signed Radbourn to a contract with Dubuque for the 1879 season. That year, the young hurler won three of the six games in which he pitched while batting .333 as a second baseman/outfielder. The performance was enough to get Radbourn a major league contract worth $750 in 1880 with the National League's Buffalo Bisons.

But Radbourn threw too much in practice and developed a sore arm. He never pitched an inning for Buffalo. He played in only six games as a position player, but after hitting just .143 he was released.

Radbourn got his arm back in shape and the following season joined Providence, where he came under the wing of legendary manager Harry Wright, whose tombstone in Philadelphia calls him "The Father of Professional Baseball." Wright was the skipper of baseball's original professional team, the Cincinnati Red Stockings organized in 1869, after which he would go on to a long and successful career in the National League.

Charley shared the pitching duties with John Montgomery Ward. In his first big league game as a pitcher, the 27-year-old rookie beat Boston, 4–2. Radbourn went on to post a 25–11 record, toiling in 41 games and 325 innings, while also appearing in 38 games as a shortstop and outfielder and hitting .219.

Through the 1885 season, Radbourn continued to make numerous appearances in the field when he wasn't pitching. But his energy was increasingly directed toward his work on the mound, and he upped his record to 33–20 in 1882. That year, he also hit an 18th-inning home run to give Ward a 1–0 victory over the Detroit Wolverines.

In 1883, Radbourn's record leaped forward again as he climbed to a 48–25 mark, starting 68 games and completing 66. Charley's 48 wins, which included a 26–0 victory over the new Philadelphia Phillies, set a National League record and comprised all but 10 of Providence's total number of victories.

Counting his eight relief appearances, Radbourn had worked in 76 of the Grays' 98 games, a condition that obviously affected the pitcher's overtaxed arm. For the 1884 season, new Providence manager Frank Bancroft decided to ease the burden carried so valiantly by Old Hoss and bring in another hurler to share the mound duties. Bancroft's choice was Charlie Sweeney, a fireballing youngster with a troublesome attitude.

The cocky Sweeney wasn't terribly interested in sharing pitching chores with Radbourn, and the two clashed repeatedly as jealousy overtook both hurlers. Once, the two nearly came to blows before being separated. Frustrated, Radbourn was ultimately suspended by the Grays after a lackluster performance in which he resorted to throwing lobs after becoming angered by the umpire's calls. Soon afterward, Sweeney, who drank heavily, struck out a then-record 18 in one game but in July left the park in the middle of a game after being relieved. He was immediately released.

Radbourn was reinstated, but he was the Grays' only pitcher. "Do you want to win the pennant?" he asked Bancroft. "Of course I do," the manager replied. "I'll pitch every game, and don't worry about my being able to do it," Old Hoss said.

Over the next three months, Radbourn pitched in 41 of the Grays' 51 games, including 30 of 32 at one point and 22 in a row. He finished the season with 60 wins, an all-time record. In one month, he won 18 straight games, another record (later broken by Tim Keefe). His 73 complete games and 678 innings are the second-highest totals in baseball history, and his 441 strikeouts rank in fourth place on the all-time list.

The Grays won the pennant, finishing 10½ games ahead of Boston. After the regular season, Providence and the New York Metropolitans of the American Association agreed to meet in what would become a forerunner of baseball's World Series. Pitching on successive days, Old Hoss started each of the first three games, completing and winning each one by scores of 6–0, 3–1, and 12–2 while allowing just 10 hits in 27 innings, striking out 16, and walking none. The series ended when New York defaulted after the third game.

In 1884, major league baseball had for the first time permitted pitchers to throw with an overhand delivery. Radbourn, who employed an unorthodox "leaping" delivery in which his feet would actually leave the ground, refused to change from his underhand style. But in 1885, his unusual kind of delivery was banned. The new rule seriously cramped Old Hoss's style. He was never again quite the same pitcher he had been.

Radbourn had a 28–21 record in 1885, giving him a five-year mark with Providence of 194–89. At the end of the '85 season, however, Providence folded. Radbourn moved to Boston, where he pitched for the next four years.

His overworked arm showing signs of weakening, Radbourn went 27–31 in his first year with the Red Stockings. In 1887, he was suspended for part of the year before coming back to post a 24–23 mark. A prolonged holdout in 1888 reduced his number of appearances to the lowest total (24) of his career and contributed to a devastating 7–16 record.

Old Hoss bounced back to go 20–11 in 1889. The following year, players in a revolt against major league owners formed their own Players (also known as Brotherhood) League. More than 100 established big leaguers jumped to the new circuit, one of whom was Radbourn. Playing with the Boston Reds, he fashioned a 27–12 record while working in 41 games, his highest total since 1887.

The Players League disbanded at the end of the 1890 season, and Radbourn returned to the National League with the Cincinnati Reds. He won 11 games (while losing 13), including the 300th of his big league career.

That special win came on June 2, 1891, when Radbourn pitched Cincinnati to a 10–8 win over Boston. Old Hoss was touched for 11 hits, but his teammates countered with 16. He struck out four and walked four to get the decision over John Clarkson.

Radbourn retired before the end of the season at the age of 36. He returned to Bloomington and sank his energy into the operation of Radbourn's Place, a saloon and pool hall he had opened a few years earlier.

In 1894, while contemplating a comeback in baseball, tragedy struck. As reported by Frederick Ivor-Campbell in the Society for American Baseball Research publication *Baseball's First Stars,* Radbourn was accidentally shot in the face by a friend while hunting. Old Hoss survived the accident, but he lost the sight in one eye, his face was badly disfigured, and he suffered partial paralysis and a loss of speech.

Too embarrassed to be seen in public, Radbourn retreated to his living quarters. He became a recluse. His wife left him, and he was seldom seen by anyone except the prostitutes with whom he consorted.

In 1897, as his health waned, Radbourn's excessive life style caught up with him. Depressed and suffering from syphilis and paresis, he began to experience convulsions. His condition deteriorated, and eventually he slipped into a coma. He died a few days later at the age of 42.

Forty-two years later, Radbourn was elected to the Hall of Fame by the Veterans Committee. It was fitting recognition for baseball's greatest 19th-century pitcher.

June 2, 1891—Reds 10, Beaneaters 8

Cincinnati	AB	R	H	Boston	AB	R	H
McPhee, 2b	5	0	1	Brodie, cf	5	1	1
Latham, 3b	4	2	1	Sullivan, lf	4	0	1
Marr, rf	5	2	2	Long, ss	2	0	0
Holliday, lf	4	4	3	Nash, 3b	5	0	0
Reilly, cf	4	1	2	Quinn, 2b	5	3	3
Keenan, 1b	4	1	2	Lowe, rf	5	0	2
Smith, ss	4	0	3	Tucker, 1b	4	3	1
Clark, c	4	0	1	Ganzel, c	4	1	2
Radbourn, p	4	0	1	Staley, p	1	0	1
				Clarkson, p	3	0	0
Totals	38	10	16		38	8	11

Cincinnati	3	0	1	0	4	0	2	0	0	–	10
Boston	0	3	1	0	2	0	1	1	0	–	8

DP–Cincinnati 1, Boston 1. E–McPhee, Clark, Long, Nash, Tucker. 2B–Marr, Tucker. 3B–Reilly, Ganzel, Quinn. HR–Latham. SB–Holliday 2, Quinn 2, Tucker, Ganzel. Earned Runs–Cincinnati 4, Boston 3. Base on Balls–Radbourn 4, Clarkson 1. Strikeouts–Radbourn 4, Clarkson 2. WP–Staley. HBP–Ganzel (by Radbourn), Sullivan (by Radbourn). W–Radborn. L–Clarkson. T–1:50. A–1,618.

John Clarkson

Thriving on Praise

There is nothing unusual about a pitcher with a personality that harbors a few abnormalities. As a breed, pitchers are known for their irregular behavior.

Some, of course, are more irregular than others. There are those who are downright eccentric. On the other end of the scale are those who might even be regarded as being pretty close to normal. The vast majority lie somewhere in between, perhaps closer to the former than to the latter, but in any case never fully lacking at least some of the quirks that go with the job.

John Clarkson fit the mold perfectly. He was a pitcher with his own special set of peculiarities.

Although he had an abundance of talent, Clarkson was no easy player to manage. Intelligent but extremely sensitive, the slender 5-foot, 10-inch, 155-pound righthander did not react well to criticism. He wouldn't pitch when he was scolded, and he withered whenever unflattering remarks were made about him.

John Clarkson won 53 games in one season and 49 in another.

Adrian (Cap) Anson, Clarkson's first big league manager, described his hurler this way in a report uncovered by Lee Allen and Tom Meany in their book *Kings of the Diamond:* "Clarkson was one of the greatest pitchers of all time, certainly the best Chicago ever had. Many regard him as the greatest, but not many know of his peculiar temperament and the amount of encouragement needed to keep him going. Scold him, find fault with him, and he could not pitch at all. Praise him and he was unbeatable."

Clarkson was by no means a basket case. He did have a lighter side, which often surfaced. One such time, he fired a lemon instead of a baseball to a batter in an attempt to demonstrate to the umpire that the game should be called off because of darkness.

When the umpire called the pitch a strike, Clarkson's point was made. The game was called.

But the dark side of Clarkson's personality always lurked nearby, and ultimately it caused his early death. According to Dick Thompson in the Society for American Baseball Research publication, *Baseball's First Stars*, Clarkson was placed in a Flint, Michigan, sanitarium with a "mental disorder" in 1905, 11 years after the end of his playing career. Described as "a hopeless physical and mental wreck," Clarkson remained in what was called an "asylum for the insane" until transferred in 1908 to the Boston area, where he was placed in a psychiatric facility. He died there one year later at the age of 47, the cause of death listed as pneumonia and general paralysis.

It wouldn't be until 54 years later that Clarkson gained long overdue admittance to the Hall of Fame, a nominee of the Veterans Committee in 1963. During a 12-year major league career, he had more than earned the spot.

In his day, few were as good as Clarkson. He had a career record of 328–178, which included seasons when he won 53 and 49 games and more than 30 four other times. His lifetime earned run average was 2.81, compiled while working in 531 games, of which he started 518, completed 485, and tossed 37 shutouts.

Clarkson struck out 1,978 and walked 1,191 while allowing 4,295 hits in 4,536 innings of work. Twice he pitched in more than 600 innings in a season, and one other time he went over 500. He led the National League in innings pitched and strikeouts four times, and in wins, games, games started, and complete games three times each.

In 1885, Clarkson fired a no-hitter, defeating the Providence Grays, 8–0. Just one month earlier, he had pitched a one-hitter against the Buffalo Bisons. He just missed another no-hitter in 1892 when Hughie Jennings of the Louisville Colonels punched a two-out single in the ninth inning for the only hit off Clarkson.

When New York Giants manager John McGraw picked his "Grand All-American Team" in 1923, Clarkson was one of his seven pitchers. "He was the most brilliant pitcher of his day," said McGraw, who had batted against the hurler in the early 1890s.

Clarkson's mostly quiet demeanor, dark good looks, and fancy off-field attire—one writer of the day called him "Beau Brumell"—helped to conceal the reality that he was such a good pitcher. But he could be especially strong-willed and calculating, and some said, very cool under fire. Some claimed he had a massive ego. And with notoriously long fingers, he threw an exceptionally nasty curve that dropped precipitously when it reached the plate.

"He could put more turns and twists into a ball than any pitcher I ever saw," said Clarkson's Chicago teammate Billy Sunday, who later gave up a mediocre baseball career to become a world-famous evangelist.

Clarkson's pitches also included a sizzling overhand fastball and a masterful change of pace, deliveries he once used to strike out seven straight batters. Pinpoint control was another one of his strengths. So, too, was his remarkable ability to study opposing hitters and learn their weaknesses, a tactic that put John far ahead of his time.

"In knowing what kind of ball a batter could not hit and in his ability to serve up just that kind of a ball, I don't think I have ever seen the equal of Clarkson," Anson said long ago.

It was Anson who had discovered Clarkson while the youngster was pitching in Michigan. Born July 1, 1861, in Cambridge, Massachusetts, Clarkson was one of five sons of a wealthy jewelry manufacturer. John's brothers Arthur (Dad) and Walter both pitched in the big leagues after attending Harvard, their combined total of 57 wins joining with their older brother's numbers to give the Clarksons the third-highest win total (after the Perrys and Niekros) for brothers in the major leagues.

Clarkson began playing baseball as a youngster, eventually performing for school teams in Cambridge. Later, he attended business school and played in semipro leagues in the Boston area. He appeared in three games with the Worcester Brown Stockings of the National League in 1882, but a sore shoulder limited his playing time. In 1883, Clarkson joined a team in Saginaw, Michigan, in the Northwestern League, and in his second year, after posting a

34–9 record by mid-August, he was spotted by Anson, who imme-diately acquired him for the Chicago White Stockings.

John won 10 and lost three the rest of the season for the White Stockings (forerunners of the Cubs). The following year, replacing the ailing Chicago ace Larry Corcoran as the bellwether of the club's staff, Clarkson had one of the greatest seasons of any hurler in major league history while leading the White Stockings to the National League pennant.

His record was a remarkable 53–16, the second-highest win total ever compiled in the big leagues and more than 60 percent of Chicago's 87 wins. Clarkson fashioned a 1.85 ERA, working in 623 innings and completing 68 of the 70 games in which he appeared. He led the league in seven pitching categories, includ-ing strikeouts (308) and shutouts (10), while twirling both a no-hit-ter and a one-hitter.

Anson switched to a three-man pitching rotation in 1886, and Chicago marched off with its sixth pennant in 11 years. Seeing less action, Clarkson worked in 466 innings but still had another sparkling season, going 36–17 with a 2.41 ERA while leading the league with 313 strikeouts and completing 50 of the 55 games he started. In another 19th-century version of the World Series, the White Stockings met the American Association champion St. Louis Browns, with Clarkson winning the first game, 6–0, but losing the third and sixth games, the latter a 4–3 decision in 10 innings of the deciding game.

Although the 1886 flag was the last one for Chicago under Anson, Clarkson continued to bewilder National League hitters in 1887 when he registered a 38–21 record while working in 523 innings and leading the league in strikeouts (237) for the third straight year. In his three full seasons in Chicago, Clarkson had won 126 of the team's 248 victories.

Clarkson's meteoric Chicago career, however, came to a stun-ning conclusion in 1888 when, for reasons never fully explained, he said he would not play again for the White Stockings. In April, the high-strung hurler was sold to the Boston Beaneaters for

$10,000. That was the same sum that Boston had paid one year earlier for Clarkson's old Chicago catcher, Mike (King) Kelly. The two were quickly nicknamed "the $20,000 battery."

Returning to his hometown, Clarkson celebrated in 1888 with a 33–20 record. He then had one of his finest seasons, going 49–19 while leading the National League in no less than 11 pitching categories, including ERA (2.73), innings (620), complete games (68), and strikeouts (284).

While he was mowing down opposing hitters with monotonous regularity, Clarkson was no slouch in other facets of the game. He was an excellent hitter, his 24 career home runs ranking him among the all-time leaders among pitchers. John was also a fine fielder who twice led the league's pitchers in assists and once recorded eight putouts in one game.

After the 1889 season, numerous National Leaguers jumped to the Players (or Brotherhood) League. But Clarkson was not one of them. His decision not to join the many other stars of baseball who switched allegiance to the new league made Clarkson extremely unpopular with a lot of the other players, many of whom shunned him for the rest of his career. Although he was accused of being bought off by Boston and of being a spy for the National League at Players League meetings, Clarkson maintained his innocence. He stayed in Boston, he said, so he could continue his job as baseball coach at Harvard.

Whatever his reasons, Clarkson continued his mound mastery. Although playing in 1890 under his third Boston manager—Frank Selee—he posted a 26–18 record. One year later, he went 33–19, combining with Kid Nichols's 30 wins to lead Boston to the National League pennant.

Boston won the flag again in 1892, but it was mostly without the help of Clarkson, who had been the Beaneaters' opening day pitcher. With a strong mound crew, Boston regarded Clarkson as excess baggage, and after posting an 8–6 mark with what was rapidly becoming a tired arm, he was sold during the season to the Cleveland Spiders.

Because of the excessive number of teams (12) in the National League that year, the season was divided into halves. Boston won the first-half title. Then Cleveland, with Clarkson going 17–10, captured the second-half crown. Thus, Clarkson, who finished with an overall 25–16 mark, played on two winners in the same season, although Boston eventually won a post-season playoff, five games to none (one tie).

During the season, Clarkson won his 300th game. On September 21, he hurled the Spiders to a 3–2 victory over the Pittsburgh Pirates. Cleveland, which had just two hits off losing pitcher Adonis Terry, scored twice in the bottom of the ninth to win, using two walks, a sacrifice, and a single. Clarkson gave up five hits while striking out three and walking two.

Clarkson spent the 1893 and 1894 seasons with Cleveland but was just below .500 each year, going 16–17 and 8–10. Even more critical, it was reported that because of his anti–Players League stance, he was so strongly disliked by his teammates that they refused to play even adequate defense on days when John was pitching.

With his fragile state of mind—weakened even more than usual after Clarkson watched in horror as a friend accompanying him on a hunting trip (Detroit Wolverines catcher Charlie Bennett) had parts of his legs severed after he slipped on ice and fell under the wheels of a train—John was in no shape to fight back. Instead, he took the only option available, retiring at mid-season.

Soon afterward, Clarkson moved to Bay City, Michigan, where he opened a cigar store and organized a local minor league team. He came East several times to coach at Harvard and Yale before his deteriorating mental health landed him in the hospital in Flint.

After Clarkson died in Belmont, Massachusetts—and was subsequently buried in the same cemetery in Cambridge where Tim Keefe would later be laid to rest—baseball writer Francis Richter of *The Sporting Life* wrote: "On all counts the deceased will always rank in history as one of the few great masters of the art of pitching." With that, no one would disagree.

September 21, 1892—Spiders 3, Pirates 2

Pittsburgh	AB	R	H	Cleveland	AB	R	H
Donovan, rf	4	0	1	Childs, 2b	3	2	1
Farrell, 3b	4	0	0	Burkett, lf	4	0	0
Miller, c	4	0	1	Davis, 3b	2	1	0
Beckley, 1b	4	1	1	McKean, ss	4	0	1
Smith, lf	4	0	0	Virtue, 1b	3	0	0
Bierbauer, 2b	2	1	1	McAleer, cf	3	0	0
Shugart, ss	3	0	0	O'Connor, rf	4	0	0
Terry, p	2	0	0	Zimmer, c	3	0	0
Kelly, cf	3	0	1	Clarkson, p	3	0	0
Totals	30	2	5		29	3	2

```
Pittsburgh    0 0 0 0 0 0 0 1 1 - 2
Cleveland     0 0 0 0 0 1 0 0 2 - 3
```

Pittsburgh	IP	H	R	ER	BB	SO
Terry (L)	9	2	3	0	5	8

Cleveland						
Clarkson (W)	9	5	2	2	2	3

E–Donovan. 2B–Beckley. 3B–Childs. SB–Davis, Beckley 2. SF–Burkett, Virtue, McAleer, O'Connor, Shugart. PB–Miller. T–1:55. A–1,300.

Kid Nichols

No Decade More Dazzling

In the unpredictable world of professional baseball, it is never fully possible to project how long it will take for a young player's real ability to surface. Some players develop quickly, some mature later on, and some never ripen at all.

But whatever the case, baseball, being the inexact science that it is, provides no sure way to make an accurate determination in advance. There is simply no way to tell when—or even if—a player will succeed.

Take the case of Charles (Kid) Nichols. The vagaries of the game were never harder at work than they were at the start of the young righthander's career. Who could have predicted that Nichols not only would launch his big league career in splendid fashion, but would have one of the best records any hurler ever had?

That was after Nichols was rejected three times in a bid as a teenager to become a professional pitcher. And it followed the

In his first 10 years in the major leagues, **Kid Nichols** won 297 games.

Kid's eventual arrival in the majors after his minor league contract had been purchased at a bargain basement rate.

By the time he retired in 1906, Nichols was hailed as one of the best pitchers ever to fling a baseball. In 15 years of National League warfare, he compiled a 361–208 record, making him the sixth winningest hurler in the game. He was the youngest pitcher ever to become a 300-game winner. He won 30 or more games in seven seasons, a major league record that still stands. He was a 20-game winner 11 times, including 10 years in a row at the start of his career.

To solidify his place among baseball legends, Nichols pitched his team, the Boston Beaneaters, to five pennants in an eight-year period. He was the biggest winner of the decade of the 1890s. And even in the twilight of his career, he returned from a two-year absence in the big leagues to win 21 games as a playing-manager with the St. Louis Cardinals.

Kid made it to the Hall of Fame in 1949, voted in by the Veterans Committee. Attending the induction ceremony with him were four generations of Nicholses. What most of them had never seen was a flame-thrower who was one of the fastest pitchers of his day.

Nichols was among the earliest of a new breed of pitcher who had grown up exclusively as an overhand thrower. Most of the other major league moundsmen of the era had been sidearm throwers who had to readjust their styles after a ruling in 1884 permitted overhand motions. Kid never had that problem because he didn't become a pitcher until after the rule went into effect.

The overhand deliveries used by the 5-foot, 10-inch, 175-pound flinger also allowed him to develop the kind of fastball that was far speedier than those thrown by most of his contemporaries. And what a fastball it was. Kid was one of the first true fastball pitchers, considered the equal of the New York Giants' Amos Rusie, the acknowledged fastest thrower of the era. Although he threw hardly anything else, Nichols had a hopping fastball that came in several different varieties. Combining that with his superb control and ability to use his head, he constantly overmatched opposing hitters.

"A pitcher must use his brain as well as his arm," Nichols once said. "A man with good control pitching to spots, an occasional change of pace, and a fast one will always get by."

Kid was also durable. He worked in more than 300 innings 12 times. Five straight times his innings exceeded 400 in a season. Overall, he pitched 5,056 innings, allowing 4,912 hits, striking out 1,873, and walking 1,268. Of the 620 games in which he appeared, 561 were as a starter and 531 were complete games, a figure that is tied for fourth place on the all-time list. He had a career 2.95 earned run average, his 2,475 runs allowed ranking sixth highest in baseball history.

Perhaps Nichols's stamina was enhanced by the absence of a big windup. Long before Don Larsen championed the no-windup delivery, Kid, who tossed 48 shutouts, including 11 by 1–0 scores, was using the technique in the 1890s.

"Many a pitcher uses an elaborate windup, and I have been repeatedly asked to adopt one," Nichols said a century ago. "I have persistently refused. I don't approve of it because it interferes with the control of the ball. It's a useless exertion on the arm, and as far as confusing the batter is concerned, it doesn't always work."

What did work for Nichols was evident as soon as he landed in the major leagues as a raw 20-year-old. Though spectacular, Kid's arrival had been sidetracked three times along the way.

Born September 14, 1869, in Madison, Wisconsin, Nichols had moved at age 11 with his family to Kansas City, Missouri. There he made the rounds of local amateur teams, achieving a degree of notoriety. When he was 16, according to Lee Allen and Tom Meany in *Kings of the Diamond,* Nichols thought he was good enough to apply for a pitching job with the local National League team, the Kansas City Cowboys. His application was rejected.

One year later, Kansas City had dropped back to the Western League, and Nichols gave the team another shot. Again, his offer was declined. A little later, however, with the team in desperate need of another pitcher, Nichols was called back. Given a contract, the 17-year-old responded by winning 18 of 31 decisions the rest of the season.

But, as reported by Bill Carle in the Society for American Baseball Research's *Baseball's First Stars,* the Kansas City management wasn't ready for their young phenom. Claiming he was still too young, the club released Nichols, who by now was being called Kid because of his youthful looks.

Kid hooked up with Memphis in the Southern League the following year and was 10–9 when the team folded at mid-season. Nichols went back one more time to Kansas City, where he finished the season with 16 wins in 18 games and a miniscule 1.14 earned run average while helping his club win the Western League pennant.

That was more than enough to get Kid a ticket in 1889 to Omaha, another Western League club. There, playing under manager Frank Selee, Nichols had one of the most sparkling seasons in minor league history. He rang up a 39–8 record with a 1.77 ERA, leading the league with 368 strikeouts and pacing Omaha to the league pennant.

That winter, Selee became manager of the Beaneaters, and although other clubs were keenly interested in the young pitcher, he made sure Nichols went with him. Boston purchased Kid's contract from Omaha for the meager sum of $3,000.

In Boston, Nichols was an instant sensation. As a 20-year-old rookie, he beat the Brooklyn Bridegrooms, late of the American Association, 5–2, in his first game. "They nicked me for two runs in the first inning, then I got mad and shut them out the rest of the way," Kid recalled.

From there, Nichols went on to post a 27–19 record, completing all 47 games he started and appearing in 424 innings in what would be the first of five straight 400-plus inning seasons.

There was no sophomore jinx for Nichols the following year. He upped his record to 30–17, establishing a career high with 240 strikeouts, and teaming with 33-game winner John Clarkson to lead Boston to its first National League pennant since 1883. Boston clinched the flag with 18 straight wins at the end of the season. There was no post-season series that year because Beaneaters management refused to meet the rival Boston Reds, winners of the American Association flag.

But the Beaneaters won the pennant again in 1892 as Nichols went 35–16 while working a career-high 453 innings and completing 49 of his 51 starts. With 12 teams in the league due to the disbanding of the American Association, the National League held a post-season playoff between first- and second-half winners, and Boston emerged the victor over the Cleveland Spiders with five wins and a tie in six games. Nichols triumphed in the fourth game, 4–0, then captured the sixth and final skirmish with an 8–3 win over Cy Young in a game in which Kid drove in the tying and go-ahead runs.

Although the mound was moved back to 60 feet, 6 inches from the plate in 1893, Nichols was unaffected, recording marks of 34–14 and 32–13. His 30-win streak was interrupted by a 26–16 log in 1895, but then he resumed his glittering run with 30–14, 31–11, 31–12, and 21–19 records, finishing his first 10 years with 297 wins, the most any hurler ever accumulated in a single decade.

Meanwhile, the Beaneaters won pennants again in 1893, 1897, and 1898, losing in '97 in four games to the Baltimore Orioles in their only appearance in the Temple Cup series, which pitted the league's first- and second-place teams. Nichols commanded a salary of $2,400 while annually ranking among the league's top pitchers. Twice Kid won three games in three days, hurling a complete game each time. And he seldom came out of a game, finishing all but 22 of the 444 games he started during the entire decade.

As the century turned, Kid was slowing down. But on July 7, 1900, he still had enough left to capture his 300th win with an 11–4 verdict over the Chicago Orphans. The youngest pitcher to reach the 300 plateau, Nichols was just two months short of his 31st birthday. Kid got the win in a 31-hit slugfest in which he and losing pitcher Nixey Callahan both went the distance, although the latter yielded 19 safeties. Boston clinched the decision by scoring seven unearned runs with two outs in the second inning. Nichols struck out two and walked two while allowing 12 hits.

Nichols finished the 1900 season with a 13–16 log, the only time he was below .500 in his career. He bounced back with a 19–16 mark the following year, but the end in Boston had finally arrived. Unwilling to accept a meager contract offer from the Beaneaters, Kid instead obtained his release and became part owner and playing-manager of the Kansas City Blue Stockings in the Western League.

Kid won 47 games for the Blue Stockings over a two-year period, sparking the team to the pennant in 1902. Across the state, the St. Louis Cardinals were watching. And in 1904, they brought Nichols back to the big leagues as playing-manager.

After being away from the major leagues for two years, Nichols celebrated his return with a 21–13 record, which included one outing when he struck out 15 Brooklyn Superbas in a 17-inning game. The Cardinals, though, finished fifth. Then 14 games into the 1905 season, Kid was fired as manager. Soon afterward, he joined the Philadelphia Phillies, beating the Cards, 2–1, in his first appearance with the team and going 10–6 to complete the season with an overall 11–11 mark.

Nichols retired at the age of 36 after pitching in four games in 1906 with the Phillies. He returned to Kansas City, where he tried his hand at several businesses, including real estate and motion pictures, a sales venture in which he was partners with former Chicago Cubs shortstop Joe Tinker.

Kid also took an interest in amateur baseball leagues and eventually became the head coach at Missouri Valley College for the 1915–16 seasons. He also got involved in bowling as manager and part owner of one of the largest alleys in Kansas City. That gave Nichols the chance to develop another career in sports.

He became one of the top bowlers in Kansas City, and in 1933 at the age of 64, Nichols won a Class A championship after rolling a 299 in the final game. Kid was still bowling when he died in 1953 at the age of 83.

July 7, 1900—Beaneaters 11, Orphans 4

Boston	AB	R	H	Chicago	AB	R	H
Hamilton, cf	5	2	2	McCarthy, lf	5	0	1
Collins, 3b	4	2	2	Childs, 2b	5	0	2
Stahl, lf	5	1	2	Mertes, 1b	5	0	4
Tenney, 1b	5	0	3	Ryan, rf	4	0	1
Freeman , rf	5	0	1	Green, cf	3	2	2
Lowe, 2b	5	1	3	Clingman, ss	4	0	0
Long, ss	5	1	2	Bradley, 3b	4	1	2
Clarke, c	3	2	2	Donahue, c	4	0	0
Nichols, p	5	2	2	Callahan, p	3	1	0
Totals	42	11	19		37	4	12

Boston	0	7	0	0	0	3	0	1	0	–	11
Chicago	0	2	1	0	0	0	0	1	0	–	4

Boston	IP	H	R	ER	BB	SO
Nichols (W)	9	12	4	0	2	2

Chicago						
Callahan (L)	9	19	11	4	1	0

DP–Boston 1, Chicago 1. LOB–Boston 7, Chicago 9. E–Lowe, Long, Bradley.
2B–Bradley 2, Collins, Tenney, Lowe. HR–Green. SB–Tenney, Green. SF–Collins.
HBP–Ryan (by Nichols), Clarke (by Callahan). T–2:12. A–4,000.

Cy Young

An Unapproachable Record

When major league baseball decreed in 1956 that forever after the best pitcher each season would be presented a special trophy, it required no degree in nuclear physics to figure out what to call the award. Just name it after the most successful pitcher who ever lived.

There could be no question who that was. Denton True (Cy) Young was the name, and extraordinary pitching feats were his game. What could be more fitting than to make the name Cy Young synonymous with baseball's best pitchers of the day?

Let statistics, the foundation of any good baseball discussion, present the case: During a glorious 22-year career, Young posted a 511–316 record. His victory total is nearly 100 more than the next highest pitcher's and represents a level that will not likely ever be surpassed, much less even distantly approached.

Young won more than 30 games five times. He won more than 20 games 15 times, an all-time record. He won more than 200

The **Cy Young** Award honors baseball's winningest pitcher.

games in each league. He pitched three no-hitters, including the first perfect game of the 20th century. He is the all-time major league leader in games started (815), complete games (749), and innings pitched (7,356). And he had more 300-inning seasons (16)

Cy Young (with Lou Criger on left) pitched in more than 300 innings in 16 different seasons.

than any other pitcher and appeared in more games (906) than any other hurler who was primarily a starter.

Longevity was Young's long suit, and because of it, he gave up more hits (7,092) than any other pitcher and the second highest number of runs (3,167). He struck out 2,803 and walked 1,217 while recording 76 shutouts and fashioning a career 2.63 earned run average. Cy led his league in shutouts seven times, in wins five times, in complete games three times, and in ERA, strikeouts, and games and innings pitched each twice.

Young was one of the first great pitchers who never had to adjust from a sidearm delivery after overhand throwing was first permitted in 1884. He grew up throwing strictly over the top. With that delivery, Young, a big strong man of 6 feet, 2 inches, 210 pounds, not only demonstrated extraordinary control, he was also extremely fast. In his early days in the major leagues, his catchers often inserted beefsteaks into their flimsy gloves to lessen the sting of Cy's fastballs.

"Speed is a decidedly bad qualification for a pitcher unless accuracy goes with it," Young once said. "I was real fast," he added, "but what very few batters knew was that I had two curves. One of them sailed in there as hard as my fastball and broke in reverse. It was a narrow curve that broke away from the batter and went in just like a fastball. The other was a wide break."

Cy, who according to one story was given that name in his early days because his blinding speed resembled that of a cyclone (another version had him getting the name because it was often what young country hicks were called), was also a thinking man's pitcher. Shrewd and knowledgeable, Young knew opposing batters and how to work them and was notorious for trying to outthink them at every turn.

With his record and talents, it is no wonder that Young was a member of the second group elected to the Hall of Fame. He entered the shrine in 1937 after collecting 153 votes out of 201 ballots cast. Sportswriter Grantland Rice called him "the greatest pitcher who ever lived."

Unlike so many older players, Young was around to see his own induction. He lived until 1955, his life ending at the age of 88 when he was stricken while sitting in a rocking chair on the porch of the Newcomerstown, Ohio, house where he resided.

Young's passing came just a few miles down the road from where he was raised in the hill country of eastern Ohio. He was born March 29, 1867, in Gilmore, Ohio, and as a youth grew strong from splitting logs and performing other heavy labors required on his family's farm. Then called "Dent," he took to baseball like a horse takes to hay, and at an early age his feats on local amateur teams were the talk of the town.

At the age of 23, Young was signed in 1890 by Canton in the Tri-State League after the team's owner, George Moreland, persuaded the young player's father to release him from his farm chores and allow him to sign a contract for $40 a month. Initially, the unsophisticated farm boy was fast but wild, and his catchers had a hard time holding him. But Young's true talent was evident, and on July 25, he fired an 18-strikeout no-hitter to run his record to 15–15. That would be Young's last minor league game. A few days later, with Canton buried in last place and suffering serious financial problems, Cy was sold to the Cleveland Spiders for $300 and a suit of clothes for Moreland.

Shortly afterward, with the Canton team having folded, Young made his major league debut with a three-hit, 8–1 victory over Cap Anson's Chicago Colts. The Chicago manager, who had been unimpressed after scouting Young at Canton, suddenly changed his tune. "That farm boy has a lot to learn," Anson said to Cleveland official Davis Hawley. "He's too green for your club, but I might be able to teach him something about pitching in a couple of years. I'll give you $1,000 for him."

Hawley was smart enough to turn down the offer. And Young went on to post a 9–7 record over the final two months of the season. The next time Cy didn't hit double figures in a season would be 20 years later.

Young went 27–22 in his first full season in the big leagues, working in his first of four straight 400-plus innings, then going 36–12 with a league-leading 1.93 ERA and nine shutouts the following year. In a post-season playoff between the 12-team National League's first- and second-half champions, the Boston Beaneaters beat the Spiders, 5–0–1, with Young working a 0–0 tie in 11 innings in the opener, then losing the third and sixth games by 3–2 and 8–3 scores.

When the mound was moved back to 60 feet, 6 inches in 1893, Cy never skipped a beat, registering a 34–16 mark. The next season, while appearing in more than 50 games for the fourth straight year, he was 26–21 before going 35–10 in 1895. That year, runner-up Cleveland, playing in the Temple Cup series, beat the first-place Baltimore Orioles, four games to one, with Young getting three wins, including a 5–4 decision in the opener and a 5–2 verdict in the clincher. The following season, when Young posted a 28–15 mark, the same teams met in the Temple Cup series, but this time Baltimore won in four straight, with Young taking a 7–1 loss in the first game.

By then, Young was well-established as one of the premier hurlers in the big leagues. His pitches were extraordinary. He had harnessed the control problems that had plagued him early in his career (in fact, he would wind up his career walking just 1.49 batters every nine innings). And he was incredibly durable. No one was stronger or had more endurance than the barrel-chested farm boy, who could grip a baseball in his hand so tightly that no one could pry it loose.

"I always had a good arm and legs," Young said in *Kings of the Diamond* by Lee Allen and Tom Meany. "You have to have good legs to pitch, and I always took care of them. When I went to spring training, I wouldn't touch a ball for the first three weeks. Just did a lot of walking and running. I never did any unnecessary throwing. I figured the old arm had just so many throws in it, and there wasn't any use wasting them. I had good control, and I aimed to make the batter hit the ball, so I made as few pitches as possible."

Unlike other flingers, Young, who claimed he never had a sore arm, rarely took more than three or four minutes to warm up before a start. When he was used in relief, he'd go directly from the dugout to the mound, never first getting ready in the bullpen. And in the off-season, he would return to Ohio and spend much of the winter chopping wood, plowing, milking the cows and doing other farm chores, and hiking through nearby hills.

His excellent physical condition allowed Young to pitch more than 400 innings five times and more than 300 innings 16 times. Until he was 42 years old, he never worked in less than 35 games in a season. Throughout his career, Cy completed 92 percent of the games he started.

In 1897, Young added another laurel to his record. Facing the Cincinnati Reds on September 18, he captured a 6–0 verdict with the first no-hitter of his career. It was the first no-hitter in the National League in four years. Cy finished the season at 21–19, then went 25–13 a year later.

That turned out to be his last season in Cleveland. When the Spiders' owners purchased a controlling interest in the St. Louis franchise, Young and some other players were shifted to the Browns. Young spent two years in St. Louis, winning 45 and losing 35 over that period, at one point tossing three straight shutouts. Then in 1901 with the formation of the American League, Cy was offered an $1,100 raise by the Boston Pilgrims and jumped to the new circuit.

Young was one of the main attractions in the new league. Hurling the Pilgrims to their first victory, 12–4, over Cleveland, he posted a 33–10 record with a glittering 1.62 ERA.

He also became the second pitcher in the 20th century to win 300 games when he topped the Philadelphia Athletics, 5–3, on July 12, 1901.

He followed that season with a 32–11 mark, then went 28–9 in 1903, along the way tossing a never-equaled three straight 1–0 victories, including the pennant-clincher that gave Boston the American League title. In the first World Series between the American and National Leagues, Young got the call as the Pilgrims' starter in the opening game against the Pittsburgh Pirates but wound up losing, 7–3. He pitched in relief in the third game, then came back to win the fifth game, 11–1, and the seventh, 7–3, as Boston won the Series, five games to three.

Now 37, Cy had another banner year in 1904 when he posted a 26–16 record with a career-high 10 shutouts. On May 5, Young became the first 20th-century hurler to fire a perfect game when he blanked Rube Waddell and the Philadelphia Athletics, 3–0. A's manager Connie Mack called it "the finest pitched game" he had ever seen. "I don't think I ever had more stuff," said Young, who struck out eight to get revenge on a foe who had bragged about how he blanked Boston earlier in the season.

Young went on to pitch a still-standing record 23 consecutive hitless innings, which included six innings of hitless relief in two games before the perfect game and six hitless innings in a start after it. He also racked up 45 scoreless innings, which included a 15-inning, 1–0 triumph over the Detroit Tigers in a game in which Cy's hitless streak was ended by Sam Crawford's seventh-inning double.

Cy, whose records for the increasingly dismal Pilgrims over the next four years were 18–19 (with 10 one-run losses and a 20-inning, no-walk outing), 13–21, 21–15, and 21–11, became the first 20th-century pitcher to fire three no-hitters when he blanked the New York Highlanders, 8–0, on June 30, 1908. A leadoff walk (on a 3–2 count) in the first inning gave New York its only base-runner of the game. At 41, the performance made Young the oldest pitcher ever to throw a no-hitter until Nolan Ryan passed him in 1990.

That same season, Boston held a "Cy Young Day," with more than 20,000 showing up for the celebration. The American League called off all other games, instead sending an all-star team to participate in an exhibition game. Cy was showered with gifts, cash, and a cup signed by many of his American League contemporaries.

Young was sold to the American League's Cleveland Naps in 1909. Commanding by now a $12,500 salary, Cy went 19–15 the first year. But with a bulging stomach and tiring arm, Young won only seven of 17 games in 1910. One of the wins was his 500th, a 5–4 decision over the Washington Nats on July 19.

During the 1911 season, Cleveland released Cy and he was picked up by the Boston Braves (formerly the Beaneaters). Late in the season, Young lost a 1–0 decision in 12 innings to the Philadelphia Phillies and their rookie pitcher Grover Cleveland Alexander. "When the kid beats you, it's time to quit," Young declared. Two weeks later, on September 22, Cy blanked Pittsburgh, 1–0, for his 511th and final win. In his final appearance, he lost to Brooklyn, 13–3, on October 6.

Young went to spring training with Boston in 1912, but his increasing size, especially around the midsection, made fielding difficult. Opposing batters had found that bunting on Cy produced easy hits. "The boys are taking unfair advantage of the old man," he said. "They know this big stomach makes it difficult to field bunts." Young retired before the season opened.

Cy, who had managed six games in Boston in 1907 as a fill-in, took a job in 1913 as skipper of Cleveland's Federal League team. The league played a six-week season. Neither Young nor the Cleveland team returned when the circuit resumed the following year, with Cy retiring to his farm.

Back in Ohio, Young occasionally played for local amateur teams. An amiable chap who was a willing conversationalist, he hung around the fringes of baseball the rest of his life, often appearing at old-timers functions and other events. One year after his death in 1955, his name once again became prominent when commissioner Ford Frick initiated the Cy Young Award. Nearly one half century after the award was originally given to one pitcher, then 11 years later was presented to the top moundsman from each league, it remains the hallmark of the excellence so brilliantly exemplified by its namesake.

July 5, 1901—Pilgrims 5, Athletics 3

Philadelphia	AB	H	PO	A	E	Boston	AB	H	PO	A	E
Fultz, cf	4	1	1	1	0	Dowd, lf	4	1	1	0	0
Davis, 1b	4	0	10	0	1	Stahl, cf	2	1	0	0	1
Cross, 3b	4	1	2	1	0	Collins, 3b	3	3	2	5	1
Lajoie, 2b	4	2	2	2	0	Freeman, 1b	2	1	11	0	0
Seybold, rf	4	1	1	0	0	Hemphill, rf	4	1	3	0	0
McIntyre, lf	4	0	1	2	0	Parent, ss	4	3	1	4	0
Powers, c	4	1	4	2	2	Ferris, 2b	3	0	4	4	0
Dolan, ss	4	0	2	6	0	Schreck, c	3	0	5	0	1
McPherson, p	1	0	0	2	1	Young, p	2	1	0	0	0
a–Smith, ph	1	1	0	0	0	Bernhard, p	1	0	1	2	0
Totals	35	7	24	18	4		27	11	27	13	3

Philadelphia	2	0	0	0	0	0	0	1	–	3
Boston	0	2	2	1	0	0	0	0	x	–	5

a–Batted for McPherson in ninth

DP–Philadelphia 2, Boston 2. 2B–Collins, Seybold. 3B–Cross, Stahl, Collins. SB–Lajoie 2, Freeman, Ferris. SF–Freeman, Ferris. Earned Runs–Philadelphia 2, Boston 1. Base on Balls–McPherson 3, Bernhard 1. Strikeouts–Young 5. HBP–Freeman (by McPherson). W–Young. L–McPherson. T–1:45. A–4,582.

Christy Mathewson

Idol of the Masses

Throughout its long and often glorious history, baseball has produced an ample allotment of players who earned the special admiration of the masses. Hero worshiping, after all, is a staple of the national pastime.

It is doubtful, however, that any player was ever more fervently idolized than Christy Mathewson. And it was a condition that wasn't restricted to just one geographic area. It extended throughout an entire nation.

Mathewson was a classic American hero, adored by fans of every stripe, hailed far and wide for his abundant qualities. Blond, blue-eyed, tall, handsome, articulate, honest, brave, moral, and hard-working, he had all the requisite virtues of an icon. Plus he could pitch.

Some claim he was the best pitcher there ever was. While that contention is arguable, there is no question that the splendid

It once took **Christy Mathewson** just 67 pitches to hurl a complete game.

righthander resides in a very special place in the pantheon of the pitching fraternity. Sportswriter Grantland Rice even went so far as to call him "the knightliest of all the game's paladins."

"In addition to physical ability," New York Giants manager John McGraw said in 1923, "he had the perfect temperament for a ballplayer. Always, he sought to learn something new and he never forgot what he learned. He had everything—strength, intelligence, courage and willingness. I give a large share of the credit for my success with the Giants to Mathewson."

Roger Bresnahan (right) said he could catch **Christy Mathewson** (left) in a rocking chair.

Mathewson's intellect was far above that of the average player of his day. A wizard at bridge and checkers, it was said that he could play a dozen different games of checkers simultaneously. In an era when players almost never went to college, Christy had attended Bucknell College for three years. He made appearances on the vaudeville stage and in several silent movies. He authored newspaper articles and made public speaking appearances. A keen student of his profession, he even wrote a rare (for that era) analytical book called *Pitching in a Pinch* in which he defined his philosophy.

"I always tried to learn about the hitters," he explained. "Any time someone got a hit off me, I made a mental note of the pitch. He'd never see that one again."

Christy's nickname was Big Six. Accounts vary regarding the origin of the name—Mathewson himself said it was a contraction for six-footer, while others claim that New York sportswriter Sam Crane first applied the term because that was the name of one of New York City's biggest and fastest fire engines. Regardless of the source, the name was so closely associated with Mathewson that he often got mail addressed simply to Big Six, New York, New York.

Despite his popularity, Big Six could be aloof and arrogant. He was stubborn and he firmly believed that all opponents were his inferior. Matty's ego was sufficiently large that on days he pitched, he had a special act. "I can see him making his lordly entrance onto the field," recalled Mordecai (Three-Fingered) Brown, who beat Christy 14 times during their long rivalry. "He'd always wait until about 10 minutes before game time, then he'd come from the clubhouse across the field in a long linen duster like auto drivers wore, and at every step the crowd would yell louder and louder."

On the mound, Mathewson had some other unusual traits. He was notorious for his reluctance to bear down all the time. Often, Christy would coast, letting batters hit the ball and only pitching hard when runners were on base or the game was close. Once, he pitched a 14-hit shutout against the Pittsburgh Pirates, going hard only when necessary. He also was one of the first pitchers to master the screwball or fadeaway, a pitch he threw only 10 to 12 times a game, but with exceptional success. Although he wasn't a strikeout pitcher, Mathewson had a swift but not overpowering fastball, a curve, and a changeup.

Control was also one of Mathewson's greatest assets. During his entire career, Big Six walked just 1.6 batters every nine innings. He walked only 42 batters in 390.2 innings in 1908. In 1913, he hurled 68 consecutive innings without a walk and, in 306 innings pitched that year, allowed just 21 free passes. "You could catch Matty in a rocking chair," Giants backstop Roger Bresnahan said.

"A pitcher needs very little power, provided he has control and uses his strength intelligently," Mathewson said. "Great speed is always prized and so is a sharp-breaking curve. If these go with good control and good judgment, they are immensely valuable, but by themselves they are worth very little. I'd rather have a pitcher who has only moderate speed and a fair curve, but who knows how to use them."

Mathewson worked in 17 big league seasons, posting a 373–188 record. His victory total is tied with Grover Cleveland Alexander as the third highest in the majors. The 6-foot, 1-inch, 200-pounder registered a 2.13 career earned run average while working in 635 games, starting 551, and completing 434, 79 of them being shutouts, a figure that ranks third on the all-time list. In 4,780.2 innings pitched, Matty yielded 4,218 hits, struck out 2,502, and walked 844.

He won 30 or more games four times and 20 or more 13 times, including a major league record 12 in a row. Matty also pitched in more than 300 innings 11 times. Five times his ERA was under 2.00. He led the National League in ERA and in strikeouts five times apiece, and in shutouts and wins on four occasions each.

Matty hurled two no-hitters. He holds the modern major league record with 37 wins in one season. He won 14 games by 1–0 scores. He once fired a complete game using just 67 pitches. And twice he won nine games in a single month.

When the initial election was held for the Hall of Fame in 1936, Mathewson was in a group of the first five players chosen, getting 205 votes out of a possible 226. Matty's selection came 11 years after he had died tragically at the age of 45.

The short life of the great hurler had begun on August 12, 1880, in Factoryville, Pennsylvania, a small town north of Scranton. The oldest of five children, Christy was the son of a developer and gentleman farmer whose family lived comfortably in a large, well-appointed house in an area where coal mines clogged the landscape.

Christy loved to throw stones, and at an early age, it was obvious that his arm was something special. That became even more apparent in high school when the youngster began pitching for Keystone Academy while also playing football and basketball. By the time he graduated, he was good enough to join a semipro team in Scranton.

That lasted only until he was lured away by a team in nearby Honesdale, which paid him $25 a month, plus room and board.

With his mother hoping he would become a preacher, Mathewson enrolled that fall at Bucknell. A fine athlete, who later shot in the 70s in golf, he became an outstanding fullback and kicker on the football team—his drop-kicking prowess so noteworthy that he was nicknamed Gun Boots—and the star pitcher in baseball, often facing a brilliant lefthander from Gettysburg College named Eddie Plank. He also participated in numerous other college activities, including the band, glee club, and literary society, and eventually became junior class president.

After a second summer with the Honesdale team, Mathewson joined Taunton, Massachusetts, in the New England League, where he posted a 5–2 record. The following summer, he moved to Norfolk in the Virginia League, where he went 20–2. Matty was then sold conditionally to the Giants but, after an unimpressive 0–3 showing, was returned to Norfolk. That winter, Matty signed for $1,200 with the Philadelphia Athletics of the new American League.

Meanwhile, the Cincinnati Reds claimed Matty from Norfolk. To make a chaotic situation even more confusing, the Reds then traded him back to the Giants for aging hurler Amos Rusie. When the Giants threatened to blackball the pitcher if he continued with the Athletics, Mathewson relented and rejoined the New York team.

Lucky for the Giants. Matty made an immediate impression in the National League as he registered a 20–17 mark in his rookie season in 1901. Included among his victories was a July 15 no-hitter against the St. Louis Cardinals in a game in which Christy struck out four and walked four while grabbing a 5–0 decision. Mathewson would toss a second no-hitter on June 13, 1905, when he beat the Chicago Cubs with a two-strikeout, no-walk squeaker, 1–0. Brown, the losing pitcher in that game, didn't yield a hit until the sixth.

Unbelievably, the year after Matty's stellar rookie season, Giants manager Horace Fogel tried to convert the young hurler into a first baseman. He had Mathewson work out there and at shortstop, using the flimsy rationale that the team would be better served if Matty's bat was in the everyday lineup. Fortunately for posterity, the misguided pilot was soon replaced by McGraw, who said Fogel's folly was "the dumbest thing I ever heard of. Get rid of him," he said. "Anybody who doesn't know any more about baseball than he does has no right in a ball park."

Mathewson, who had promised his mother that he wouldn't play baseball on Sundays, a vow he never broke, slipped to 14–17 in 1902. It would be the last time he was under 20 wins until 1915.

Matty went on a 30-win binge, posting records of 30–13, 33–12, and 31–9 over the next three years. In 1903, he set a career high with a league-leading 267 strikeouts. The following year, he fanned 16 Cardinals in a 3–1 win. And in his best season ever in 1905, he led the league with a dazzling 1.28 ERA while capturing his third straight strikeout crown.

That fall, Mathewson added to his already glittering reputation when he fired three shutouts against the Athletics in a memorable World Series in which the opposition was blanked in all five games. He beat Plank, 3–0, in the first game with a four-hitter, breezed to a 9–0 triumph with another four-hitter in Game Three, then won the fifth and final game with a six-hit, 2–0 decision over Chief Bender. In 27 innings, Matty struck out 18 and issued just one walk in what would go down as the finest pitching performance in World Series history.

Following his Series heroics, Matty went back to dominating National League hitters. He logged 22–12 and 24–12 records before exploding to 37–11 in 1908. The 37 wins established a modern major league record that still stands. That season, Christy beat the Cardinals for the 24th straight time, while leading the league in virtually every major pitching category, including strikeouts (259), shutouts (11), ERA (1.43), innings pitched (390.2), and complete games (34).

Matty continued his torrid pace with 25–6, 27–9, 26–13, 23–12, 25–11, and 24–13 records between 1909 and 1914. He won his 300th game during the 1912 campaign with a 3–2 decision over the Cubs on June 13 at the Polo Grounds. Christy struck out eight and walked one while yielding six hits, getting the best of Larry Cheney in a tight pitchers' duel. After a triple by Tommy Leach led off the bottom of the ninth for the Cubs, Mathewson retired the side to preserve the win.

Mathewson never again scaled the heights of his 1905 World Series achievements. In eight other starts, he won just twice, including a 2–1, six-hit victory over Bender and the A's in the first game of the 1911 World Series. He lost 3–2 in the third game and 4–2 in Game Four of the Athletics' six-game victory that year. In 1912 when the Giants fell to the Boston Red Sox in an eight-game Series, Mathewson pitched 11 innings in a 6–6 tie called by darkness in Game Two, dropped a 2–1 decision in the fifth game despite retiring 17 in a row, and bowed, 3–2, in the eighth game made famous by the fielding blunders of Fred Snodgrass and Fred Merkle, which led to two Red Sox runs in the bottom of the ninth inning. Matty topped Plank, 3–0, in the second game of the 1913 Series but dropped a 3–1 decision to his old college rival in the fifth and deciding game in what would be his final World Series appearance.

In 1912, Mathewson was earning the princely sum of $10,000. Two years later, when the Federal League was formed, he was offered a reported $65,000 for three years if he'd jump to the new circuit. Matty picked loyalty over flattery and stayed with the Giants.

His career, though, was on a downward spiral. In 1915, with little left in his once-great pitching arm, Big Six was relegated to part-time duty in the bullpen, and his record fell to 8–14. In mid-season the following year, with just three wins in 12 games, Matty was approached about managing the Cincinnati Reds. The Giants obliged by trading him in a five-player swap, and Mathewson took over the reigns on July 20. The Reds went 25–43 the rest of the way, finishing last. Matty made one final appearance on the mound, beating his old nemesis Brown and the Cubs, 10–8.

Mathewson guided the Reds to a 78–76 mark and a fourth-place finish in 1917, then had his club in the same spot with a 61–57 mark the following year when he abruptly resigned to accept a commission as a captain in the Army. With the United States having entered World War I, Matty was assigned to the chemical warfare division and soon thereafter was on his way to France.

A bout with the flu marred Matty's voyage across the ocean. More seriously, though, once he got to France, Christy repeatedly inhaled lethal mustard gas while instructing recruits in sealed training facilities in the correct way to wear gas masks. Mathewson's lungs suffered permanent damage.

While he was still in Europe after the war, the Reds had tried to reach Mathewson to advise him that his old job was waiting for him. When Matty never replied—because he never got the message—the Reds hired Pat Moran as manager.

Matty's health was not good anyway. He spent time in a hospital but seemingly recovered enough to take a job in 1919 as a coach with the Giants. But he could not overcome a persistent cough, and gradually his health deteriorated. Diagnosed as having tuberculosis, he moved with his family to a prominent sanitorium on Saranac Lake in the Adirondack Mountains in New York.

Eventually, Matty's health improved. Thinking he was cured, he left the sanitorium and, against doctors orders, went back to work. Investing $300,000 in the Boston Braves, Mathewson took a job in 1923 as president and part owner of one of his old National League rivals.

Big Six ran the club for more than one year, but ultimately the work wore him down and his health regressed. The cough returned, he had trouble breathing, and he suffered severe pain. Matty returned to Saranac Lake. On October 7, 1925, his body ravaged by tuberculosis, he died there at the age of 45. His passing was mourned by an entire nation of loyal admirers.

June 13, 1912—Giants 3, Cubs 2

Chicago	AB	R	H	New York	AB	R	H
Sheckard, lf	3	0	1	Devore, lf	4	0	0
Schulte, rf	4	0	0	Doyle, 2b	4	1	3
Downs, ss	4	0	0	Snodgrass, 1b	3	0	1
Leach, 3b	4	0	1	Murray, rf	3	0	1
Miller, cf	4	0	1	Becker, cf	3	0	1
Saier, 1b	4	0	1	Herzog, 3b	3	1	1
Evers, 2b	4	1	1	Myers, c	2	1	2
Archer, c	3	1	1	Fletcher, ss	2	0	0
Cheney, p	3	0	0	Mathewson, p	3	0	1
Totals	33	2	6		27	3	10

Chicago	0	0	0	0	1	0	1	0	0	–	2		
New York	0	0	0	0	2	1	0	0	x	–	3		

DP–Chicago 1. E–Devore, Schulte. LOB–Chicago 5, New York 4. 2B–Myers, Mathewson. 3B–Leach. HR–Archer. SB–Becker, Doyle. SF–Snodgrass. SFF–Fletcher, Murray. Base on Balls–Cheney 1, Mathewson 1. Strikeouts–Cheney 5, Mathewson 8. T–1:45.

Eddie Plank

A Hitter's Nightmare

Two things can be said about Eddie Plank with undeniable certainty. He was the first great lefthanded pitcher of the 20th century. And he was a man who specialized in being unconventional.

Plank not only won more games than any other southpaw during the first decade of the century; he was baseball's winningest lefty until the 1960s. Even today, he holds the all-time records for most shutouts (69) and most complete games (410) by a lefthander, and the American League mark for most wins (305) by a southpaw.

While winning 20 or more games in eight different seasons and reaching a career total of 327 victories, Plank carved a niche that put him among the finest of baseball's pitching legends. He achieved baseball's highest honor when he was elected posthumously to the Hall of Fame in 1946.

"He was a pitcher who combined a rare knowledge of his opponent's weakness and had marvelous control," Connie Mack, Plank's

Eddie Plank won his first game at the age of 25 after never having pitched in the minors.

manager with the Philadelphia Athletics, once said. The pitcher was a "combination of good temperament, savvy, control, and courage," A's captain and second baseman Eddie Collins claimed. "He was not the fastest, not the trickiest, and not the possessor of the most stuff," Collins told baseball writer Harry Grayson. "He was just the greatest."

Plank also marched to the beat of his own drummer. A solemn, serious loner who it was said "had no sense of humor," Plank was neither colorful nor popular with teammates, fans, or sports writers. He seldom joined teammates after games, and he tended to have little to say to those around him.

"Eddie was a steady, capable workman, but he was quiet and self-effacing," said Ed Pollack in a long-ago column in the

Philadelphia *Evening Bulletin.* "Except when pitching assignments put him in the public eye, he was in the background, shrinking away from the spotlight."

Before pitching each time, Plank insisted on being served a bowl of tomato soup. Once he got to the mound, he worked so slowly and consumed so much time between pitches that batters, his own fielders, and even fans were alienated.

"He would fuss and fiddle with the ball, with his shoes, with his cap, his belt, his shirtsleeves, then he'd try to talk to the umpire," Collins recalled. "Then he'd throw over to first three or four times. Finally, he'd turn his attention to the fretting batter, whose concentration had long since been broken. He'd do that on every pitch."

Plank's dilly-dallying style made him one of baseball's greatest time-consumers. "He would stand on the mound so long that your eyes would water between pitches," one anonymous hitter told Tom Meany in *Baseball's Greatest Pitchers.* So annoying were his habits, it was once said that fans who came to games on commuter trains wouldn't come on days when Plank pitched because they feared missing their trains home.

Eddie also had the habit of talking to himself on the mound. "Nine to go," he'd say in a loud voice as the seventh inning began. "Eight to go," he'd announce after retiring the first batter. "I had trouble getting used to that," Mack said. "He did it all the time. But whenever I'd say something about it to him, he'd just glare at me."

When he was finally ready to deliver the ball, Plank would rock back and forth, the batter never knowing when the ball would be released. That, of course, was all part of Plank's strategy to keep the batter off balance. Ultimately, the ball would zoom toward the plate, one of a variety of pitches that the 5-foot, 11-inch, 175-pound portsider had in his arsenal.

Plank, who had a nasal problem that made breathing difficult, threw hard, although not as hard as teammate Rube Waddell. He also employed a crackling curve. And he had an assortment of other pitches that he used to keep opposing hitters off balance, all

Despite many years with the A's, **Eddie Plank** won his 300th game as a Federal Leaguer.

delivered with a sidearm motion that seemed to come from somewhere in the vicinity of first base.

"They shouldn't allow that Plank to pitch from first base," said a frustrated Josh Devore after one particularly grueling day at the plate. "He's tough enough when he stays on the mound."

Plank's excellent control was reflected in his having walked just 1,072 batters in 4,495.1 innings. In 17 years, Eddie, who struck out 2,246 while allowing 3,958 hits, averaged just 63 walks per season. Although he seldom led the league in any pitching category, his career record was 327–194 with an earned run average of 2.34 in 623 games, including 529 as a starter.

Fifteen of Plank's seasons were spent with the Athletics. In that period, the A's won six American League pennants as Eddie joined Waddell, Chief Bender, and Andy Coakley in the early years, then Bender and Jack Coombs in later years to give Philadelphia some of the finest starting rotations ever assembled. Waddell and Bender are also in the Hall of Fame.

Eddie was a late bloomer. He didn't join the Athletics until he was 25 years old, and he arrived with no minor league experience. Born August 31, 1875, on a farm near Gettysburg, Pennsylvania, Plank played baseball as a boy in the fields. His first encounter with an organized team came when he entered Gettysburg Academy, a local high school. In 1896, when he was 21, Plank enrolled as a freshman at Gettysburg College. Although big and strong, and in possession of a blazing fastball, he knew little of the art of pitching. Gradually, however, he developed, and in due time he turned into a brilliant college hurler.

Gettysburg often faced nearby Bucknell College, and frequently the opposing pitchers were Plank and another up-and-coming youngster named Christy Mathewson. In every one of their meetings, Mathewson got the decision.

Plank's college coach was Frank Foreman, whose brother Brownie had pitched briefly for Connie Mack at Pittsburgh in the 1890s. A former major league hurler and friend of Mack, too, Frank Foreman repeatedly wrote to Mack, proclaiming the talents of his sparkling hurler. At the time, Mack was assembling a new team in preparation for the first season of the newly formed American League. Eventually, Mack gave in, heeding the advice of his old friend and signing Plank sight unseen to a contract.

One of the first college players to enter the major leagues, Plank would not report to his new team until he earned his degree. When he finally arrived, however, he was everything Mack had hoped for.

"From day one, I knew that fellow would do well for me," Mack said. "He had those sharp features, a jutting jaw, well-defined lines, and a hard-nosed attitude. He was dead serious about his pitching, and he was a thinking man as well."

Plank wasted little time making an equally good impression around the rest of the league. Two days after his arrival, he won his first start, beating the Washington Nationals, 6–4. He lost his next decision but then reeled off eight straight victories. Despite never having worked an inning in the minors, Eddie finished his rookie season with a 17–13 record.

Over the next six years, Plank was a 20-game winner five times, including 26–17 in 1904, 24–12 in 1905, and 24–16 in 1907. Possibly his best year of the six was in 1906, when he went 19–6 in a season in which Eddie saw reduced action because of arm trouble.

Five times during that period, Plank toiled in 300 or more innings a season, reaching a high of 357 in 1904. Four times he started 40 or more games, twice leading the league in that category. "He was just a wonderful pitcher," Mack said.

After each season, Plank returned to his home in Gettysburg, where he worked his family's 100-acre farm, helping to grow crops, breaking in broncos, and even delivering milk from the sizeable herd of cows on hand. And if that wasn't enough, Eddie also served as a guide at the nearby Civil War battlefield.

Plank's success during the season was sharply contrasted by his lack of success in the four World Series in which he played, although the results were to a great extent not of his own doing. Eddie won just two of the seven games in which he pitched, but four of his five losses came when the Athletics were shut out.

In the Athletics' first World Series appearance in 1905 (there was no Series in 1902 when they also won a pennant), Plank was a 3–0 loser to Mathewson and the New York Giants in the opening game and was outdueled, 1–0, by Joe McGinnity in Game Four, despite pitching a four-hitter. That Series, won by New York, became famous because all five games were shutouts.

Arm trouble knocked Plank out of the 1910 Series, but he split two decisions in the 1911 event in which the A's beat the Giants in six games. Eddie twirled a five-hitter to beat Rube Marquard, 3–1, in Game Two, then lost the fifth game, pitching in relief in the 10th inning, 4–3. Plank lost again to Mathewson, 3–0, in the second game of the 1913 Series before coming back to beat his old adversary, 3–1, on a two-hitter in the fifth and deciding game. Eddie's final decision came in the 1914 Series when he was defeated, 1–0, by Bill James in Game Two of a Boston Braves sweep.

In seven World Series games totaling six complete games and 54.2 innings of work, Plank gave up just 36 hits and 11 runs. His ERA was 1.32.

There were many other noteworthy games during Plank's career. In 1908, while Frank Smith was pitching a no-hitter for the opposing Chicago White Sox, Eddie lost, 1–0, in the ninth when Freddy Parent reached out while being intentionally walked and poked a game-winning sacrifice fly to right. The following year, Plank won the first game played at Shibe Park, beating the Boston Red Sox, 8–1. In 1912, he pitched all 19 innings of a 5–4 loss to Washington in what was then the longest major league game to date. He once flirted with a no-hitter, giving up a scratch single to the Washington Senators' Eddie Foster in the ninth inning.

Plank posted a 23–8 record in 1911, a 26–6 mark in 1912, then won 33 over the next two years. After winning 285 games for the Athletics between 1901 and 1914, Plank was released by the Athletics when Mack decided to break up the splendid team that had given him four pennants in the last five years. Plank signed with the St. Louis Terriers of the one-year-old Federal League, a circuit established to compete with the existing major leagues.

The 39-year-old southpaw still had something left. Although the competition was not on a par with the American League, Eddie registered a 21–11 record. During the season, he gained his 300th victory on August 28—just three days short of his 40th birthday—beating the Kansas City Packers, 3–2, on a five-hitter. Plank struck out two and walked four, hurling a shutout until the seventh inning, when a couple of errors helped the losers score twice.

Harmony returned to baseball and the Federal League disbanded after the 1915 season. Plank landed back in the American League with the St. Louis Browns. He went 16–15 in 1916 and told friends, "I wouldn't be surprised if I'm pitching in baseball when I'm 50 years old." But the following year after 20 games and a 5–6 record, the quiet lefty decided he had had enough. Plank went home to his farm.

That winter, the Browns traded Plank and second baseman Del Pratt to the New York Yankees for five players, including Urban

Shocker, a top-level hurler. When Plank refused to report, saying he was sticking to his retirement plans, Yankees manager Miller Huggins offered the 43-year-old hurler a three-year contract. Plank turned it down.

Plank resumed his small-town life, opening an auto business, helping his parents on the farm, hunting, and taking part in local activities, including some stints on the mound with a local independent team. That tranquility, however, was shattered in 1926 when, at 50 years of age, Plank suffered a paralyzing stroke. Within a few hours, he was lapsing in and out of consciousness. Newspaper reports carried detailed descriptions of his condition, advising readers that there was no hope for the ex-pitcher's recovery.

Plank died three days after being stricken. His passing came just four months after his great rival, fellow Pennsylvanian Christy Mathewson, had died in an equally tragic way.

August 28, 1915—Terriers 3, Packers 2

Kansas City	AB	R	H	St. Louis	AB	R	H
Chadbourne, cf	4	0	0	Tobin, cf	4	0	2
Kenworthy, 2b	4	0	1	Vaughn, 2b	4	1	1
Kruger, lf	3	0	0	W. Miller, lf	4	1	1
Perring, 1b	4	0	0	Borton, 1b	4	0	0
Bradley, 3b	4	1	1	Hartley, c	4	0	0
Gilmore, rf	2	0	0	Drake, rf	3	0	1
Rawlings, ss	4	1	1	E. Johnson, ss	3	1	1
Easterly, c	3	0	1	Bridwell, cf	1	0	0
Henning, p	3	0	1	Plank, p	2	0	0
a–Brown, ph	1	0	0				
b–Enzenroth, ph	0	0	0				
Totals	32	2	5		29	3	6

Kansas City	0 0 0 0 0 0 2 0 0 – 2
St. Louis	0 0 1 2 0 0 0 0 x – 3

a–Batted for Easterly in 9th
b–Batted for Henning in 9th
DP–St. Louis 2. E–Bradley, Rawlings, Easterly, Hartley, E. Johnson, Bridwell. 2B–Kenworthy, Vaughn, Henning. SB–Vaughn, W. Miller, E. Johnson. SF–Bridwell, Kruger, Plank. Base on Balls–Henning 1, Plank 4. Strikeouts–Henning 2, Plank 2. T–1:54.

Walter Johnson

Fastball Was Fearsome

The list of great fastball pitchers always starts with Walter Johnson. Others make the roster. But when it comes to speed, no one delivered a pitch any swifter than the man sometimes called The Big Train.

Johnson had two speeds: fast and faster. With long arms, a smooth, easy style, and pitches that were whipped from an uncomplicated sidearm motion, Walter served up a steady diet of fireballs that over a 21-year period spent entirely with the Washington Senators often left opposing hitters feigning illness so they didn't have to play when he pitched. "The thought of facing Walter's fast one upset their digestion," wrote renowned sportswriter Ring Lardner.

The 6-foot, 1-inch, 200-pound powerhouse didn't bother much with a curve. He just threw fastballs. And he made little attempt to conceal them. Batters knew they were coming, but it

Many consider **Walter Johnson** to be the greatest pitcher of all time.

made no difference. Laying a bat solidly on a Johnson pitch was like trying to ascend the Washington Monument on a bicycle.

"He was the fastest righthanded pitcher who ever lived," said Philadelphia Athletics manager Connie Mack. Added New York Yankees outfielder Whitey Witt: "He had one of the greatest arms God ever put on a man. His speedball came up, and it looked like a golf ball coming at you. If he hit you, he'd have killed you."

When the great Ty Cobb batted against the big righthander the first time, he reported that Johnson was so fast, it scared him. "I hardly saw the pitch, but I heard it," he said. "It just hissed with danger. We knew we'd just met the most powerful arm ever turned loose in a ballpark." Cobb immediately urged Tiger management "to get this kid even if it costs $25,000."

Cobb was just one of many hitters who regarded Johnson as the fastest pitcher in baseball. Tris Speaker, Joe Jackson, Nap Lajoie, and Babe Ruth did, too. Once, while batting against The Big Train, Ruth argued a called third strike. "I thought that sounded a little low," he protested.

Eddie Collins was also on the bandwagon. "Walter Johnson is without question the greatest pitcher of all time," he said in a statement that to this day remains indisputable. Famed sportswriter Grantland Rice, who nicknamed Johnson The Big Train because of his flaming fastball, said, "Year in and year out, he was the hardest man to beat that ever sent a ball flashing over the plate."

Johnson's magnificent fastball, of course, translated into strikeouts. Walter fanned 3,509 during his career, a big league record that stood until 1983. Seven times, he whiffed more than 200 in a single season, and twice he went over 300. He also had exquisite control. He walked just 1,363 in 5,914.1 innings, never passing 100 batters in any season.

Although often anchored by the weight of weak teams—10 times, his Senators finished in the second division—Johnson was still able to win more games than any pitcher except Cy Young. He posted a 417–279 record along with a 2.17 earned run average, the lowest for any pitcher with more than 200 wins. Perhaps the most amazing of Johnson's accomplishments was the fact that more than one-quarter of his wins were shutouts. His 110 whitewashes represent one of the most unapproachable major league records in the book.

Overall, Johnson pitched in 802 games, starting 666, and completing 531. He gave up 4,913 hits, well under one per inning. He was later credited with 34 saves. He fired a no-hitter and seven one-hitters. He won a major league record 38 1–0 games and made 14 opening-day starts (winning nine, seven being shutouts). He once pitched 55.2 consecutive scoreless innings, had a 16-game winning streak, and in 1916 went the whole season without giving up a home run in 369.2 innings of work.

In addition to ones already mentioned, Johnson is among the all-time leaders in numerous other categories. He faced more batters (21,663) than any pitcher in big league history. He is third in innings pitched, and fourth in complete games, 200-inning seasons (18), losses, and hit batters (206). Among his many American League records, he holds marks for most wins, most losses, most games pitched with one club, most starts, and most complete games. He also lost 65 games when his team was shut out.

Johnson entered the Hall of Fame in the first group ever elected. He was chosen in 1936 with 189 votes of the 226 ballots cast.

A gentle, kind-hearted man with a sunny disposition and an even temperament, Johnson refused to throw at batters or even to brush them back. That allowed hitters to dig in at the plate. It mattered little. Walter still dominated hitters with the ease of a king ruling his subjects.

Once asked to reveal the secret of his success, the self-effacing Johnson had a predictable answer. "You must love baseball," he said. "A man must live and breathe the game every minute of his waking hours."

Johnson's success made him the most idolized pitcher of the 1920s. And in Washington, D.C., where eminent figures have occasionally towered above the scandals and scoundrels, no one ever stood taller than Walter. He was the essence of distinction in the nation's capital.

Walter—he was never called Walt—was the quintessential American hero. A model citizen with small-town values, he was called an inspiration for clean living, loyalty, and sportsmanship. He neither smoked, drank, nor swore, he didn't argue with umpires, and he never blamed a teammate for a mistake. In an era when ballplayers were known for their rough edges, Johnson offered a sharp contrast. He was a man of such high character that he was admired on as well as off the field.

The character of the noble Walter began to take shape at an early age. He was born on a farm on November 6, 1887, in Humboldt, Kansas, the son of "salt-of-the-earth" parents who

Walter Johnson led manager Bucky Harris's Washington Senators to two pennants.

taught their five children strong values and common sense. As a youth, Johnson demonstrated an ability to throw a baseball with remarkable speed, but it wasn't until the family moved to California in 1902 that his prowess attracted attention.

By the age of 16, Johnson was not only playing with his local high school team in Fullerton but also was pitching with a semipro team. Eventually, after a brief stint with a minor league team in Tacoma, Washington, the youngster landed in Weiser, Idaho, where he pitched on weekends for the local semipro team and dug postholes for a railroad during the week.

According to most reports, Johnson and his blazing fastball were spotted by a traveling cigar salesman, who wrote glowing accounts of his discovery to several big league managers, including Joe Cantillon of the Senators. Cantillon sent injured catcher Cliff

Blankenship out to scout the youngster. Astounded by what he saw, Blankenship soon had Johnson on a train heading for Washington, despite the efforts of the Weiser residents to keep him by offering to set him up with his own cigar store.

Johnson made his big league debut on August 2, 1907, losing, 3–2, to the hard-hitting Detroit Tigers, who quickly learned they could bunt on the raw rookie. Afterward, the naïve 19-year-old, unaware that there was a team bus, walked back to the hotel in his uniform. Along the way, a man pointed to the nearby Johnson Hotel and told the young pitcher that it had just been named after him. Walter joyfully believed the lie.

Five days later, Johnson won his first game, a 7–2 decision over the Cleveland Naps. With only one pitch—a fastball—he ended the season with a 5–9 record, despite a 1.88 ERA, his first of 11 times under the 2.00 mark. His record was elevated to 14–14 in 1908, a year in which he blanked the New York Highlanders three times in four days, allowing 12 hits in 27 innings. Walter slipped to 13–25 the following year, losing 10 games when the lowly Senators failed to score a single run.

Possessor of remarkable stamina, Johnson launched a streak in 1910 in which he pitched at least 300 innings in nine straight years. That year, he set career highs in innings pitched (370) and complete games (38) while registering a 25–17 record, the first of 12 times he won 20 or more games. He also won his first of 12 strikeout titles with a career-high 313.

Although somewhat out of character for him, Johnson staged a holdout in 1911. When he settled just before the season began, he signed a three-year contract for $7,000 a year. It was a bargain for the Senators. Walter posted 25–13, 33–12, and 36–7 records over that period, the best three years of his career. In the middle of the three years, he set a modern record with 16 straight wins.

The following year, when he won a career-high 36 games, was the best of Johnson's career. He captured his second of five ERA titles with an astounding 1.14 and at one point hurled 55.2 consecutive scoreless innings, a mark that stood until 1968. He led the league with 11 shutouts. In 346 innings of work, Walter walked just 38 batters. Late in the campaign, Washington fans presented him with a silver cup filled with $10 bills. At the end of the 1913 season, Johnson was named winner of the Chalmers Award, the equivalent of today's MVP.

Always in the public eye, Johnson achieved another kind of notoriety in 1914 when he married Hazel Roberts, a 19-year-old debutante and daughter of Nevada congressman Edwin E. Roberts. Walter celebrated his good fortune with a 28–18 season. At the end of the campaign, though, a different kind of experience surfaced. The one-year-old Federal League tried to lure the Big Train to Chicago with a contract offer of $16,000, plus a $6,000 bonus.

Johnson gave the offer serious consideration. But with his friend Cobb urging him to turn it down and Washington owner Clark Griffith threatening a lawsuit, he finally rejected the deal, returning to the Senators and a new contract worth $12,500 a year.

Over the next five years, Johnson went 27–13, 25–20, 23–16, 23–13, and 20–14, establishing himself as the finest pitcher in baseball history. Twice, he beat George Sisler, a fledgling pitcher with the St. Louis Browns who would become a Hall of Fame first baseman. He also pitched against Ruth eight times, losing six of those games, three by 1–0 scores. In 1918, Walter went 18 innings to beat the Chicago White Sox, 1–0. And in 1919, he retired 28 batters in a row in a 12-inning game with the New York Yankees.

Barney, a nickname given to Johnson because his fast driving reminded passengers of race-car driver Barney Oldfield, had unquestionably his most incongruous season in 1920. On May 14, he won his 300th game, beating the Tigers in relief, 9–8, at Griffith Stadium. Walter worked the last three and two-thirds innings, yielding three hits and no runs before the Senators pushed over one run in the bottom of the ninth.

Less than two months later, Johnson finally got a no-hitter when on July 1 he blanked the Boston Red Sox, 1–0. Only an error by second baseman Bucky Harris prevented Walter's masterpiece from being a perfect game. Shortly afterward, Johnson, who struck out 10 and walked none, came down with a sore arm and pitched no more games that season, ending with an 8–10 record.

Although Johnson won only 49 games (losing 42) over the next three years, he still had some big games left. In 1924, his 23–7 mark, which included a seven-inning, rain-shortened no-hitter against the Browns and 14 straight victories, at long last led Washington to its first American League pennant. In the World Series against the New York Giants, the nearly 37-year-old legend lost both the opener, 4–3 in 12 innings, despite 12 strikeouts, and the fifth game, 6–2. In the seventh game, however, with the score tied 3–3, Johnson emerged from the bullpen in the top of the ninth and proceeded to pitch four scoreless innings. He finally got the win in the 12th inning when Earl McNeely's grounder hit a pebble and bounced over the head of Giants third baseman Freddy Lindstrom to let the winning run score for Washington.

Johnson, named the league's MVP in 1924, got the Senators back in the Series in 1925 with his last 20-win (20–7) season. He also hit .433 that year. Walter's 7–0 victory over the Athletics— the 23d time he'd blanked the A's—put Washington in first place to stay in late June. Johnson fanned 10 and yielded just five hits to beat the Pittsburgh Pirates in the Series opener, then hurled a six-hit shutout to win Game Four, 4–0. In the seventh game, however, Walter, weary and playing with an injured leg, was battered for 15 hits and wound up a 9–7 loser as the Pirates won the Series.

The Big Train beat the Athletics, 1–0, in 15 innings in the 1926 opener. Later, Walter won his 400th game with a 7–4 decision over the Browns. But he finished the season at 15–16. Then, with time having extracted a heavy toll on his aging arm, and having broken a leg in spring training, the 39-year-old hurler tumbled to 5–6 in 1927. Walter retired at the end of the year.

But Johnson was hardly through with baseball. He managed the Newark Bears of the International League in 1928, the team posting an 81–84 record and finishing seventh. That fall, Johnson signed a three-year contract to return to the Senators as manager.

He piloted the team for four seasons, compiling an overall 350–264 mark, which included one second- and two third-place finishes. Walter was let go by the Senators after the 1932 season but landed with the Cleveland Indians. He skippered the Indians for three years, going 179–168 with two third-place and one fourth-place finishes. He resigned during the 1935 season, writing an end to a managerial career during which he registered a 530–432 record in seven seasons.

Johnson, who lived in Coffeyville, Kansas, during his playing career, bought a 535-acre farm in Germantown, Maryland, where he would live the rest of his life. After retiring from baseball, he dabbled in different occupations, working in public relations, briefly appearing as a Senators broadcaster, and trying his hand at politics. He served as a county commissioner, then ran a losing race in 1940 for Congress. Twice during World War II, he pitched to Ruth in exhibitions at Yankee Stadium that raised in excess of $100,000 in war bonds.

Johnson died of a brain tumor at the age of 59 on December 10, 1946. Eulogies described him as the greatest pitcher who ever lived. They were not exaggerating.

May 14, 1920—Senators 9, Tigers 8

Detroit	AB	R	H	Washington	AB	R	H
Young, 2b	4	1	1	Judge, 1b	5	0	1
Bush, ss	2	1	0	Milan, lf	4	0	1
Cobb, cf	5	0	1	Rice, cf	4	2	2
Veach, lf	4	0	3	Roth, rf	1	3	0
Heilmann, 1b	3	1	1	Harris, 2b	5	2	1
Flagstead, rf	4	2	1	Ellerbe, 3b	4	1	3
Hale, 3b	4	1	1	Shannon, ss	4	1	3
Jones, 3b	1	0	0	Garrity, c	2	0	0
Stanage, c	2	0	1	Zachary, p	2	0	0
b–Pinelli, pr	0	1	0	Erickson, p	1	0	0
Ainsmith, c	1	0	0	Johnson, p	2	0	2
Glaisier, p	2	0	0				
a–Shorten, ph	0	1	0				
Oldham, p	0	0	0				
Dauss, p	1	0	0				
Totals	33	8	9		34	9	13

Detroit	0	1	0	2	0	5	0	0	0	–	8
Washington	3	0	0	0	3	0	2	0	1	–	9

a–Batted for Glasier in 6th.

b–Ran for Stanage in 6th.

DP–Detroit 1. LOB–Detroit 8, Washington 12. E–Young, Rice, Garrity 2. 2B–Veach 2, Harris, Stanage. SB–Judge, Harris 2, Ellerbe, Heilmann, Flagstead. SF–Roth, Heilmann 2, Garrity 2, Bush, Rice. Base on Balls–Glaisier 5, Zachary 2, Erickson 4, Oldham 2, Dauss 1. Strikeouts–Glaisier 2, Zachary 2, Erickson 1, Oldham 1. Hits off–Zachary 5 in 4 IP, Erickson 1 in 1 1/3 IP, Johnson 3 in 3 2/3 IP, Glaisier 7 in 5 IP, Oldham 2 in 2/3 IP, Dauss 4 in 2 1/3 IP. Winning Pitcher–Johnson. Losing Pitcher–Dauss. T–2:35.

Grover Cleveland Alexander

From Triumph to Tragedy

One of the most naturally gifted pitchers ever to climb to the top of a major league mound was a slender righthander who answered to the quaint name of Grover Cleveland Alexander. He was also one of the most tragic.

Alexander entered the world as the namesake of the sitting U.S. President. Two years after he departed, a future U.S. President played the pitcher in a movie about his life. But there was nothing presidential about the 6-foot, 1-inch, 185-pound hurler—except when he gripped a baseball.

When he did that, he was a true chief executive, and hitters became merely hapless members of the proletariat. Alexander ruled with a combination of talent, confidence, and strong will. At his peak, nothing could veto the presentations he made from the mound.

Over one three-year period, **Grover Cleveland Alexander** posted a 94–35 record.

He was called Alec or Alex in his early days, and then Pete or Ol' Pete later on. Whatever name he went by, Alexander was one of baseball's greatest hurlers. And he achieved that distinction with spectacular conquests in both the dead and live ball eras.

"Just to see Pete out there on the mound with that cocky little undersize cap pulled down over one ear, chewing away at his tobacco and pitching baseballs as easy as pitching hay is enough to take the heart out of a fellow," Babe Ruth said.

Throwing sidearm and with an abbreviated motion, Alexander had a small stride and a smooth, effortless delivery that gave the appearance that he was hardly exerting himself. Batters knew otherwise. Although not a strikeout pitcher, Alexander had a blistering heavy, sinking fastball and an assortment of curves that broke in varying directions and to varying degrees. "I consider my curve ball my main strong point," he once said. "I have pretty good speed and a good change of pace, but the main thing with me is curves."

So good was Alexander's breaking ball that he was said to have been the only pitcher to throw curves on pitchouts. "That's because his curve was easier to hang on to," said catcher Bill (Reindeer Bill) Killefer. "His fastball was apt to tear my mitt off."

Alexander also had magnificent control. He seldom offered a hitable pitch, mostly nibbling at the corners of the plate and keeping the ball low. "He could pitch into a tin can," said the noted sportswriter Grantland Rice. "His control was always remarkable—the finest I have ever seen."

As fine as he was on the mound, Alexander was just the opposite off it. Although a pleasant, likeable fellow personally, much of his career—as well as his post-baseball life—was hampered by a severe drinking problem. He also suffered from epilepsy. He was married twice to and divorced twice from the same woman. After baseball, he lived in near poverty, drifting from one town to the next, working low-level jobs, living in rooming houses, drinking himself into oblivion, and often winding up in a jail or a hospital—a pathetic figure who tried but who could never succeed in regaining the dignity his life once embraced.

Years earlier, it had been a life that put Alexander at the top of his profession. Confirmation of that came in 1938 when he entered the Hall of Fame in the third year of balloting. He collected 212 votes out of a possible 262.

Alex's credentials were impeccable. He had a career record of 373–208, his winning total tying with Christy Mathewson as the third highest in big league history. He had a career earned run average of 2.56. He appeared in 696 games, starting 600 and completing 437, 90 of them being shutouts, which ranks second to Mathewson on the all-time list. In 5,190 innings, Alexander gave up 4,868 hits, struck out 2,198, and walked just 951. He also was later credited with 32 saves.

Alexander's complete game total is the most for any National League pitcher in the 20th century. His career ERA is the lowest for any National Leaguer with more than 200 wins. He led the league in shutouts and in innings pitched seven times apiece, in wins, strikeouts, and complete games each six times, and in ERA five times, each time with a figure below 2.00.

During a 20-year career spent with the Philadelphia Phillies, Chicago Cubs, and St. Louis Cardinals, Alexander won a NL record 17 games by 1–0 scores. He tossed five one-hitters and was opening-day pitcher 12 times (winning eight). Three times he won 30 or more games, and on nine occasions he won 20 or more. He worked in more than 300 innings in nine different seasons and in more than 200 innings 15 times.

Alexander lived for the days when he pitched, and he didn't mind sharing with others his feelings for the game, as revealed by Jack Kavanagh in his book *Ol' Pete*. "I love baseball," he said. "I always have. I'd like to play from morning 'til night. Too many fellows think of how much they are going to get for pitching. When a man doesn't love to play baseball for the game's sake, he's handicapped."

Ol' Pete hurled many games of note, but none attracted more attention than his performance in the final game of the 1926 World Series. Toiling for the Cardinals against the New York Yankees, the 39-year-old pitcher had fired a complete game, 10–2,

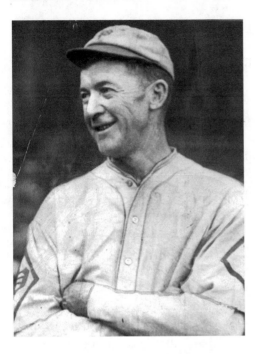

Pete Alexander joined the Cubs after an ill-advised trade by the Phillies.

victory the previous day, before which he had won Game Two, 6–2. Now, with the Series tied, Jesse Haines drew the starting assignment for St. Louis in the seventh game. But with the knuckleballing Haines's finger torn apart with broken blisters, the bases loaded with two outs in the seventh inning, and the Cardinals holding a 3–2 lead, manager Rogers Hornsby summoned Alexander from the bullpen. Alec proceeded to strike out hard-hitting Tony Lazzeri on four pitches, then blanked the Yanks the rest of the way to give the Cards the Series.

Stories immediately surfaced that Alec had gone on a drunken binge to celebrate his win the night before, that he was hung over, that he was sleeping in the bullpen when called, and after being shaken awake and without benefit of a warm-up stumbled to the mound bleary-eyed and foggy. Alexander always denied the charges. "I don't want to spoil anyone's story," he said, "but I was cold sober. There are stories that I celebrated the night before and had a hangover, but that isn't true. I was as sober as a judge." Given the tense circumstances of the situation, Ol' Pete's account seemed much more credible than the fictional tale that has been carried over the ages.

By then, Alexander was already a 300-game winner. He had passed that magic mark on September 20, 1924, when he hurled the Cubs to a 7–3, 12-inning victory over the first-place New York Giants at the Polo Grounds. Although he allowed 15 hits, Alex went the distance, striking out five and walking one. The Cubs, who had 16 hits, clinched the win with four runs in the 12th with the help of five singles and a Giants error.

Alexander had started on the long and often troubled path to that lofty plateau in Elba, Nebraska, where he made his first appearance on February 26, 1887. One of 13 children (five of whom died in infancy), he was the son of a corn farmer and as a boy developed strength by performing the requisite chores around the property.

The freckle-faced, redheaded kid grew into a tall, brawny teenager who played on local baseball teams around nearby St. Paul, Nebraska. While also working at a job digging postholes for a telephone company, he began attracting the attention of scouts. In 1909, he signed a contract with Galesburg (Illinois) of the Illinois-Missouri League.

At Galesburg, Alec had a 15–8 record when in mid-season a shortstop's throw on a double-play ball hit him in the head as he slid into second base. Unconscious for 36 hours, Alexander finally awoke to find he had double vision. His team, however, told no one, instead selling him to the American Association team at Indianapolis.

That winter, after realizing that it had been sold damaged goods, Indianapolis peddled Alexander to Syracuse. But the pitcher's vision cleared up, and in 1910 he posted a 29–14 record with the New York State League team. During one stretch, he yielded just one unearned run over 87 innings.

The Phillies bought Alexander's contract for the bargain price of $750, and in 1911, the 24-year-old hurler made his major league debut with a 5–4 loss to the Boston Braves. Soon afterward, he won his first game, a 10–3 decision over the Brooklyn Dodgers, and Alec was off to the races.

In one of the most brilliant seasons ever staged by a rookie, Alexander went 28–13, leading the league in wins, complete games, innings pitched, and shutouts, which included four in a row. He struck out 227, a rookie record that stood until 1984. No freshman hurler has ever come close to his 28 wins or to such a spectacular overall performance.

Alexander followed up with 19–17, 22–8, and 27–15 seasons, each time working in more than 300 innings, a feat he accomplished in each of his first seven seasons. But the best was yet to come. In 1915, the ex-Nebraska farm boy posted a 31–10 record with a brilliant 1.22 ERA to lead the Phillies to their first pennant in club history. Alec fired four one-hitters during the season while leading the league in numerous categories, including a career-high 241 strikeouts. His final one-hitter came as the Phils clinched the pennant with a 5–0 victory over the Braves.

Naturally, Alexander pitched the World Series opener. He beat the Boston Red Sox, 3–1, allowing eight singles. The Phillies would not win another World Series game until 1980. The slump included a 2–1 loss in Game Three when, despite another masterpiece, Alec was beaten by Duffy Lewis's two-out single in the bottom of the ninth. In that game, the Phils' hurler strained his side and was unable to pitch again in the Series, a condition that obviously contributed to Philadelphia's loss in five games.

The 1915 season, however, launched Alexander on one of the most remarkable runs in pitching annals. The rangy righthander went 33–12 in 1916 and 30–13 the following year, giving him three straight 30-win seasons and a three-year mark of 94–35. Only one National League pitcher since then (Dizzy Dean in 1934) has won 30 games in a single season.

Over that three-year period, Alex walked just 172 batters in 1,152.2 innings. Even more amazing, Alexander registered a record 16 shutouts in 1916, including five blankings of the Cincinnati

Reds, one of them a 1–0 game that was played in 58 minutes. That year, he also had career highs in innings pitched (389), complete games (38), and starts (45), and a 1.55 ERA, his second of six straight years of ERAs under 2.00. In 1917, he beat the Dodgers in both ends of a doubleheader at Ebbets Field, 5–0 and 7–3.

Incredibly, Alexander's marvelous record was achieved while the Phillies played at dingy Baker Bowl, a ballpark where the distance down the right field line to the wall was just 272 feet. Equally incredible, Alec was traded to the Cubs after the 1917 season in a four-player deal that netted the Phillies $60,000 and two useless players. Phils miserly owner William Baker said that with World War I raging, he was afraid Alexander would be drafted into military service.

Baker was right. Alex pitched three games for the Cubs in 1918, then went into the Army. Eventually, he spent nearly eight months on the front line in France, loading shells into canons and ducking the return fire of the enemy. When he came home, he was a different person.

Alexander had developed a taste for booze before he left. Now, his habit had become more serious. Alex was turning into an alcoholic. Moreover, the epilepsy which had only occasionally appeared began to surface more frequently. He was starting to look much older than his years, and he preferred to be left alone to drink.

After going 16–11 in 1919, Ol' Pete had his last great year in 1920 with a 27–14 mark while leading the league in ERA (1.91), strikeouts, innings pitched, complete games, and starts. He won 31 games over the next two years, went 22–12 in 1923, then won 30 more games before the Cubs sold him to St. Louis for $6,000 during the 1926 season after new manager Joe McCarthy got tired of Alexander's bouts with the bottle.

The great hurler, whose uniform always looked too tight and his cap too small, gave the Cardinals a 21–10 season in 1927 and a 16–9 log the next year, although he took a battering in the World Series, lasting less than three innings in a 9–3 loss to the Yankees in Game Two. He drew a fine salary of $17,500. But Alexander's drunken antics got him released after the 1929 season. He returned to the Phillies in 1930 with nothing left except memories. After nine games, the Phillies released the 43-year-old hurler.

Tired Ol' Pete tried to hook on with Dallas in the Texas League but lasted only briefly.

He then joined a traveling semipro team called the House of David, an outfit noted for its bearded players. Alec pitched beardless for the team for several years but eventually became so ineffective that even it didn't want him.

Alexander spent the rest of his life a gaunt, forlorn shadow of his former self. "I had control of everything but myself," he said. "I've laughed as many times as I've cried, so I guess I'm even with life."

He couldn't hold a job, moved from one town to another, and despite the caring efforts of his off-again, on-again wife Aimee, could never conquer his alcoholic fervor. He hit rock bottom in the early 1940s when he went to work at a flea circus on Times Square, a demeaning job in which he sat in an old chair and talked to fans who remembered his good days. "It's better living off the fleas than having them live off you," Alex rationalized.

Sam Breadon, owner of the Cardinals, sent Ol' Pete a monthly check of $100 to help pay his rooming-house rent. Often, either from an epileptic seizure or in a drunken stupor, the ex-pitcher would fall, get hurt, and wind up in a hospital or sometimes a jail.

Thirty-five years after he gave the Phillies their first pennant, Alec attended the club's second trip to the World Series. One month later, he died alone in a rooming house back where it all began, in St. Paul.

In 1952, a movie called *The Winning Team* was made about Alexander's life. The pitcher who was named after a U.S. President was played by Ronald Reagan, a future U.S. President. It was the final ironic twist to a life that had gone from triumph to tragedy.

September 20, 1924—Cubs 7, Giants 3

Chicago	AB	R	H	New York	AB	R	H
Adams, ss	7	1	1	Lindstrom, 3b	4	0	1
Heathcote, cf	4	1	2	O'Connell, 3b	2	1	0
Grantham, 2b	5	0	1	Frisch, 2b	6	1	2
Fitzgerald, c	6	1	1	Nehf, rf	0	0	0
Friberg, 3b	5	1	3	Youngs, rf	5	0	3
Grigsby, lf	5	3	1	Kelly, cf	6	0	3
Hartnett, c	6	0	4	Terry, 1b	6	1	0
Cotter, 1b	6	0	2	Wilson, lf	6	0	2
Alexander, p	6	0	1	Jackson, ss	6	0	3
				Gowdy, c	5	0	0
				Barnes, p	2	0	0
				a–Southworth, ph	1	0	0
				Jonnard, p	0	0	0
				b–Bentley, ph	1	0	1
				c–McQuillan, pr	0	0	0
				Ryan, p	0	0	0
				d–Snyder, ph	1	0	0
				Maun, p	0	0	0
				Baldwin, p	0	0	0
Totals	50	7	16		51	3	15

Chicago	0	1	0	0	0	1	1	0	0	0	4	–	7	
New York	0	0	1	0	0	0	0	1	1	0	0	–	3	

a–Batted for Barnes in 7th.

b–Batted for Jonnard in 9th.

c–Ran for Bentley in 9th.

d–Batted for Ryan in 11th.

DP–Chicago 1, New York 1. LOB–Chicago 12, New York 13. E–Adams, Heathcote, Grantham, Friberg, Hartnett, O'Connell, Kelly, Jackson. 2B–Wilson. 3B–Hartnett. SB–Frisch. SF–Heathcote, Grantham. Base on Balls–Barnes 1, Ryan 2, Alexander 1. Strikeouts–Jonnard 2, Barnes 1, Ryan 2, Alexander 5. Hits off–Alexander 15 in 12 IP, Barnes 10 in 7 IP, Jonnard 0 in 2 IP, Ryan 1 in 2 IP, Maun 3 in 1/3 IP, Baldwin 1 in 2/3 IP. Winning Pitcher–Alexander. Losing Pitcher–Maun. T–2:30.

Lefty Grove

Hot-Tempered Fireballer

There was never any question about Lefty Grove's ability as a pitcher. The only question concerning one of baseball's greatest left-handed hurlers was which generated more heat, his fastball or his temper.

Both were legendary. Both were frightfully nasty. And both produced such sizzling temperatures that they terrified mere mortals.

Although no devices existed in his day to measure the speed of pitches, Grove's fastball is regarded as one of the quickest ever delivered. No less an authority than Babe Ruth once said it was "just as fast as a rifle shot." Catcher Mickey Cochrane said that Grove was so fast, "he could throw a lamb chop past a wolf." And the great second baseman Charley Gehringer claimed that when Grove threw his fastball, "by the time you'd make up your mind whether it would be a strike or a ball, it just wasn't there anymore."

Philadelphia
American League

No 20th-century pitcher ever had a better season than **Lefty Grove**'s 31–4 in 1931.

Opposing batters often claimed that Grove's pitches arrived at the plate too quickly for umpires to see them. "That pitch sounded high," batters would lament. Joe Sewell once said that when the sun was out, Grove's fastball "looked like a flash of white thread coming at you."

Grove relied almost entirely on his fastball during the first nine years of his major league career when he was the mainstay of the Philadelphia Athletics pitching staff. "He didn't have a curve," said teammate Roger (Doc) Cramer. "All he had was a fastball. Everybody knew what they were going to hit at, but they still couldn't hit him. He was fabulous."

With his blazing fastball, Grove led the American League in strikeouts in each of his first seven years, a feat only Dazzy Vance also accomplished. Once, Grove struck out Lou Gehrig, Ruth, and Bob Meusel on nine pitches. Another time, he fanned Gehrig, Ruth, and Tony Lazzeri on 10 throws, one being a foul ball.

As scorching as his fastball was, though, Grove's temper was just as hot. His tantrums were frequent and volcanic. No clubhouse was safe after a Grove loss. Grove destroyed or rearranged furniture and anything else that stood in his way in virtually every clubhouse in the big leagues.

If he made a mistake, no teammate was immune to Lefty's wrath. Once, after making an error that resulted in a Grove loss, Boston Red Sox playing-manager Joe Cronin was subjected to such post-game abuse that he had to lock himself into his cubicle. "He used every obscenity in the book, and a few I'd never heard before," Cronin said.

When asked once by a writer to describe some of the funny incidents he'd encountered in baseball, Grove, according to Lee Allen and Tom Meany in *Kings of the Diamond,* responded gruffly, "I never saw anything funny about the game."

In his riveting book, *Lefty Grove, American Original,* Jim Kaplan reports that Connie Mack once said, "I took more from Grove than I would from any man living." Grove frequently directed profanity-laced tirades at his manager that today would have resulted at the very least in heavy fines. Once, he even fired his glove at Mack. The normally unflappable Connie picked it up and heaved it back, striking Grove in the side of his head.

Possibly Grove's most famous tirade occurred in 1931 when he lost a 1–0 game to the St. Louis Browns while going for what would have been his 17th straight win. The defeat came when reserve out-fielder Jim Moore—filling in for an injured Al Simmons—mis-played a fly ball that led to the winning run. While ripping off his uniform and sending buttons flying in every direction and knock-ing down clubhouse partitions, Grove uncharacteristically ignored Moore, attacking instead Simmons for missing the game and man-ager Connie Mack for giving him the day off.

Despite his hellacious temper, Grove was never thrown out of a game and never had a fight with an opponent. "He was a careful tantrum thrower," Ted Williams once said. "When he punched a locker, he always did it with his right hand. And he'd kick a water bucket with the side of his foot, not with his toes. But, boy, what a pitcher he was. He was the smoothest, smartest pitcher I ever saw. He had beautiful style and a beautiful motion."

Lefty had the statistics to prove it. While working 17 years in the big leagues—the final eight with the Red Sox—he rang up a 300–141 record, giving him the seventh best winning percentage (.680) in baseball history. His career ERA was 3.06, and in 616 games, he worked 3,940.2 innings, yielding 3,849 hits, striking out 2,266, and walking 1,187. Grove completed 298 of the 457 games he started, with 35 of them being shutouts.

Often used in relief between starts, primarily during his days with the Athletics, Grove was eventually credited with 55 saves. He had a 33–22 record coming out of the bullpen.

Grove was a 20-game winner eight times, his best season being in 1931 when his 31–4 mark made him not only the American League's Most Valuable Player, but the league's last 30-game winner until Denny McLain in 1968. He led the league in ERA nine times, a total uncontested in big league annals, in winning percentage five times, in wins four times, and in complete games three times.

Lefty Grove is congratulated by Jimmie Foxx (right) after getting his 300th win.

The slender 6-foot, 3-inch, 190-pound hurler never took an especially scientific approach to the art of pitching. "It never mattered to me who was up there," he said. "Whenever things went against me, I just worked that much harder." All he wanted to do was to get the batter out, and he focused on that task with incredible intensity.

Robert Moses Grove did not grow up with the unquenchable desire to be a baseball player. He didn't even play much as a youth. Born in the western Maryland coal-mining town of Lonaconing on March 6, 1900, Grove quit school at an early age and eventually wound up with a job in a silk mill, earning 50 cents a day.

Young Bob wanted nothing to do with the coal mines where his father and four brothers worked. He continued to work in the silk mill for several years, ultimately getting up to a salary of $7 a week. Eventually, he left the silk mill to work in a glass factory, where he earned the lofty sum of $5.25 a day.

Grove, who said later that he developed his strong arm throwing rocks, played some sandlot ball, where he performed mostly at first base because no one could catch his sizzling fastball. But after attracting attention while playing with an amateur team in nearby Midland in 1919, Grove signed a contract for $125 a month with Martinsville, a team in the Blue Ridge League. He didn't last long there, though, soon attracting the attention of the Baltimore Orioles, owned and managed by Jack Dunn, the same man who discovered Babe Ruth.

Needing money for a fence to border the outfield of its new field, the Martinsville club sold Grove's contract to Baltimore for an amount various reports say was either $3,000 or $3,500. Grove was an immediate success. The gangly, untutored, and unsophisticated small-town kid went 12–2 in half of a season. Over the next four years, he posted a combined record of 97–34, winning 27 twice and 25 once and leading the fast-paced International League in strikeouts each year. The Orioles won the pennant all five years, and by Grove's fifth year, he was commanding the high salary of $7,500.

Although big league teams clamored for Grove's services, Dunn steadfastly refused to sell his star hurler. Finally, however, after the 1924 season, he relented, peddling Grove to Connie Mack and the Athletics for $100,600. Dunn insisted that Mack add the extra $600 so the sale would break the all-time baseball record of $100,000 that the New York Yankees had paid to purchase Babe Ruth from the Red Sox.

Initially, Grove was a bust. The 25-year-old rookie struggled with his control and with his temper, he knew nothing about the ways of the big city, he was inarticulate and impatient, and he was a shy loner off the field who had trouble making friends with his teammates. Worst of all, he couldn't win consistently. He went 10–12 in his first season and 13–13 in his second, although he led the league in strikeouts each time and in ERA his sophomore season.

To the rescue came veteran catcher Cy Perkins, a backup backstop who had been in the league since 1914. Perkins took the young upstart under his wing, and eventually some of his wisdom began to rub off. Most importantly, Perkins got Grove to slow his pace on the mound, convincing the pitcher to work more deliberately and with greater composure.

Grove's career began to take off. Starting with a 20–13 mark in his third season, Grove put together seven straight 20-win seasons, topped by a 28–5 mark in 1930 and his 31–4 in 1931. The '31 season, for which Grove was paid $25,000, is regarded as one of the greatest any pitcher ever had. He led the league with a career-low 2.06 ERA, 27 complete games, 175 strikeouts, and an unimaginable .886 won-lost percentage while working in 41 games (30 as a starter) and 288.2 innings.

Over a four-year period between 1930 and 1933, Lefty compiled a 108–27 record, leading an Athletics pitching staff that with Rube Walberg and George Earnshaw is considered one of baseball's better starting rotations.

While throwing little else but a fastball, Grove terrorized enemy hitters, who feared permanent injury should one of Lefty's blazers go astray. "I was naturally wild enough to give them something to think about," Grove recalled, "but I never threw at a hitter. If I ever hit a guy in the head with my fastball, he'd be through. I knew that, and the hitters knew that."

"Mose" or "Groves," as Mack called him, led the Athletics to American League pennants in 1929, 1930, and 1931, the first two also World Series victories for the A's. Curiously, Mack, who was never averse to making some unfathomably bad decisions during his excessive managerial reign, used Lefty in just two relief appearances in the 1929 World Series. Grove split the decisions in two starts and won a second game in relief in the '30 fall classic, while winning twice and losing once in three starts in the '31 Series.

"In many ways," said an effusive Mack, "he is the best left-handed pitcher I ever saw." That was high praise from a manager whose rosters had included southpaw Hall of Famers Eddie Plank, Rube Waddell, and Herb Pennock.

During the 1932 and 1933 seasons, Grove won 49 games, but following the latter, he was sold with Max Bishop and Walberg to the Red Sox for $125,000 as Mack continued the dissipation of his last great team. Grove developed arm trouble in his first year in Boston and was a major disappointment. But with his fastball disappearing, he developed a curve and eventually a forkball, and in 1935 he rebounded with a 20–12 record while leading the league in ERA.

As mostly a crafty, breaking-ball pitcher, Grove then went 63–29 over his next four seasons in Boston, three more times leading the league in ERA and at one point winning a record 20 consecutive home games. All the while, he was creeping closer to the coveted 300-win mark, a plateau he was determined to reach.

With time running out, Grove, now called "Old Mose," won only seven games in 1940. He entered the 1941 season at the age of 41 needing seven more wins to become the first hurler in 17 years to win 300.

Pitching once a week during a season made famous by Joe DiMaggio's 56-game hitting streak and Ted Williams's season-ending .406 batting average, Lefty won his 299th game on July 3, beating the Athletics, 5–2, to raise his record to 6–2. Grove lost his next two starts before facing the Cleveland Indians on July 25 at Fenway Park.

The Indians jumped out to a 4–0 lead, but two-run homers by Jim Tabor in the fourth and Williams in the fifth tied the score. Lou Boudreau gave the Indians a 6–4 lead with a home run in the seventh before Tabor's homer pulled Boston to a 6–6 tie in the bottom of the inning. Then Grove's best friend in baseball, Jimmie Foxx, laced a two-run triple in the eighth to put Boston ahead to stay. A few minutes later, Grove, exhausted but thrilled, finished the ninth with a 10–6 victory and his long-sought 300th win. Grove, who could have been removed at several points had the Red Sox not been determined to see him get the verdict, gave up 12 hits, struck out six, and walked one.

Starting six more times, Grove lost three decisions and never won another game, retiring at the end of the season. He returned to his home in Lonaconing, where mellowed and devoid of the fire that had made him such a fierce competitor, he lived quietly, running a bowling alley, taking an active role in youth baseball, and briefly serving as police chief until moving to Norwalk, Ohio, in his later years. Grove died in 1975, 28 years after he was elected to the Hall of Fame with 123 of the 161 ballots cast.

July 24, 1941—Red Sox 10, Indians 6

Cleveland	AB	R	H	RBI	Boston	AB	H	R	RBI
Boudreau, ss	5	2	3	1	DiMaggio, cf	4	1	0	0
Rosenthal, cf	4	1	1	0	Finney, rf	4	1	1	0
Walker, lf	4	1	2	1	Cronin, ss	4	2	0	0
Heath, rf	4	2	2	1	Newsome, ss	0	0	0	0
Keltner, 3b	4	0	2	1	Williams, lf	3	3	2	2
Trosky, 1b	2	0	1	0	Spence, lf	0	0	0	0
Mack, 2b	1	0	0	0	Foxx, 1b	3	1	1	2
Grimes, 2b, 1b	4	0	0	1	Tabor, 3b	4	2	3	4
Desautels, c	3	0	1	0	Doerr, 2b	5	0	0	0
a–Hemsley, ph	1	0	0	0	Peacock, c	3	0	2	1
Krakauskas, p	2	0	0	0	Grove, p	4	0	1	0
Harder, p	1	0	0	0					
Milnar, p	0	0	0	0					
b–Bell, ph	1	0	0	0					
Totals	36	6	12	5		34	10	10	9

Cleveland	0	1	3	0	0	0	2	0	0 – 6
Boston	0	0	0	2	2	0	2	4	x – 10

a–Batted for Desautels in 9th.

b–Batted for Milnar in 9th.

LOB–Cleveland 4, Boston 9. E–Trosky, Mack, Grimes, Williams. 2B–Keltner 2, Boudreau, Grove. 3B–Walker, Foxx. HR–Boudreau, Tabor 2, Williams. SB–Boudreau, Heath. SF–Finney. Base on Balls–Krakauskas 4, Harder 2, Milnar 2, Grove 1. Strikeouts–Krakauskas 3, Harder 1, Milnar 1, Grove 6. Hits off Krakauskas, 1 in 3 IP, Harder 6 in 3 2/3 IP, Milnar 3 in 1 1/3 IP. Winning Pitcher–Grove. Losing Pitcher–Milnar. T–2:27. A–16,000.

Warren Spahn

The Complete Package

It takes all kinds of pitchers to make a world. Then there was Warren Spahn. The masterful lefthander was in a class by himself.

One look at Spahn, and it was obvious that he was something special. He carried himself with a kind of stylish, confident grace that screamed of success. And then when he threw a pitch, there was no question—here's a guy who has what most other pitchers only wish they could have.

Spahn may have been the most complete pitcher ever to put his fingerprints on a baseball. There was nothing he couldn't do—and do well. He could throw with speed. He could throw with finesse. He had control. He was tough. Disciplined. Intelligent. A brilliant analyst, a thinking pitcher who always knew what he was doing. And he could hit, field, run the bases, and he had one of the best pickoff moves to first base there ever was.

Warren Spahn is the winningest lefthander of all time, with 363 victories.

The slender 6-foot, 175-pound hurler was also the greatest left-handed pitcher ever to lace on a pair of spikes. Others may lay claim to that distinction. But none toiled as successfully or for as long a time as the fun-loving, amiable Spahn.

"He's beyond comparison with any modern lefthander," Casey Stengel once said. "He has beaten every handicap—the live ball, second-division teams. No one can ever say anything to deny his greatness."

Others agreed. "I thought Spahn was the greatest pitcher I ever saw," said Hall of Fame contemporary Robin Roberts. "The toughest pitcher is the one who can break the ball either way—into or away from you—and that's what Spahn did," said Stan Musial.

So reliable was Spahn that manager Chuck Dressen once referred to him as "a go-to-sleep pitcher. I mean," explained Dressen, "a manager knows Spahn's going to pitch tomorrow, so he gets a good night's sleep. He doesn't have to stay up late thinking. He knows Spahn will do all the necessary thinking." Added another former skipper, Gene Mauch: "He thinks like a manager out there." Teammate Johnny Sain called Warren "one of the smartest men ever to play the game."

Spahn reduced the art of pitching to its basic elements. Love the game. Work hard. Stay in shape. Take the job seriously. Use your head. Know the hitters. Never give them anything good to hit. And have at your disposal an assortment of outstanding pitches.

Warren threw a hard fastball, curve, and changeup in his early days, then when his speed began to falter, he developed a devastating screwball and a slider. He rarely threw a ball across the middle of the plate. In addition to his arm, one of Warren's biggest assets was his keen mind. He constantly sought ways to get the upper hand. "Hitting is timing," he said. "Pitching is upsetting timing."

"If I had to describe myself," Spahn said, "it might be a complex picture because it changed from year to year. I was never satisfied with what I did the year before. I always wanted to improve. I'd go to spring training every year with something in mind to accomplish. It was dedication. Concentration. I always wanted to be one step ahead of the hitters.

"Pitching is nothing more than unadulterated hard work," he added. "That goes for every phase of pitching." Of course, it helped that he enjoyed his work. "Baseball to me is more of a love than a job," said Spahn, who never had a sore arm.

With his career record of 363–245, compiled during 21 years in the major leagues, Spahn won more games than any lefthander in baseball history. He recorded more 20-win seasons (13) than any other southpaw, and he holds the all-time major league records for

In 1948, **Warren Spahn** helped the Boston Braves win their first pennant since 1914.

most times leading his league in wins (eight) and in complete games (nine). He also registered more complete games (382), more shutouts (63), pitched more innings (5,243.2), and worked more 200-inning seasons (17) than any other lefthanded National League hurler.

In 750 games overall, including 665 starts, Spahn posted a 3.09 earned run average, allowing 4,830 hits, striking out 2,583, and walking 1,434. Warren led the league in strikeouts and innings pitched, each four times, and in ERA on three occasions. He also gave up more home runs (434) than other National League hurler and has the second-highest total of losses for a lefthander. Only three pitchers hit more home runs than Spahn's 35. And he started 82 double plays, a major league record for a pitcher.

During a career spent almost entirely with the Boston and Milwaukee Braves, the durable portsider tossed two no-hitters. He won one Cy Young Award and narrowly missed winning three others. And he was a member of 14 All-Star teams.

Such glittering achievements made Spahn an easy choice for the Hall of Fame. He entered the baseball shrine in 1973, attracting 315 votes out of a possible 380.

One of the biggest games of the lefty's career had come 12 years earlier when on August 11, 1961, at Milwaukee's County Stadium, he beat the Chicago Cubs, 2–1, for his 300th win. Warren, who yielded six hits while striking out five and walking one, had broken a scoreless tie in the fifth with a sacrifice fly. The Cubs tied the score in the sixth, but Gino Cimoli broke the deadlock with an eighth-inning home run that gave Spahn and the Braves the victory.

"This was the toughest, most exciting game I ever pitched," said the 40-year-old Spahn, who had won his 299th game one week earlier with a 2–1 decision over the San Francisco Giants. "The game was built up to a great degree. I couldn't help but feel it."

Remarkably, Warren didn't win his first major league game until he was 25 years old. By then, he had traveled a curling path that included valorous service during World War II.

Spahn joined the human race April 23, 1921, in Buffalo, New York. His first name was chosen because it was the same as that of the nation's president, Warren G. Harding.

Warren's father, Edward, a wallpaper hanger and weekend ballplayer, began training his son to play baseball at an early age. Initially, the youngster was a first baseman, but in high school he turned to pitching and in his last two years won every game he started.

Cornell University offered Spahn a part scholarship, but his family couldn't afford the remaining costs. Instead, the skinny southpaw signed a contract in 1940 for $80 a month with the Boston Braves, at the time the only team that had shown any interest in him. Warren was sent to Bradford (New York) in the Pony League, where he was 5–4 in 12 games. He then went 19–6 at Evansville (Three-I League), good enough for an invitation to spring training with the Braves.

In an exhibition game in 1942, Stengel, then Boston's manager, ordered Spahn to brush back the Brooklyn Dodgers' Pee Wee Reese. When the young lefty didn't do it, an angry Stengel sent him to Hartford (Eastern League), where Warren posted a 17–12 mark before rejoining the Braves at the end of the season.

With war raging abroad, Spahn was soon drafted. Entering the Army as a private, Warren emerged three years later as a first lieutenant after earning a battlefield commission for heroic duty with the 276th Engineer Combat Battalion. He also was awarded a Purple Heart and a Bronze Star.

Considerably matured by his military experiences, Spahn rejoined the Braves in 1946. He won his first major league game on June 14 before finishing the season with an 8–5 record. That would be his last year under double figures until 1964.

Spahn soared to a 21–10 record in 1947 while leading the league in ERA (2.33), innings pitched (289.2), and shutouts (seven). The following year, although his record slipped to 15–12, Warren teamed with his roommate Sain to lead the once-lowly Braves to their first National League pennant since 1914. The work of the two hurlers gave birth to the slogan "Spahn and Sain and pray for rain," a suggestion—although somewhat illusionary—that Boston had no other reliable starters. In the World Series, Spahn lost Game Two, 4–1, then won the fifth game, 11–5, with five and two-thirds innings of one-hit, scoreless relief. The Braves lost the Series the following day, four games to two.

Over the next three years, as the Braves drifted back toward mediocrity, Spahn posted records of 21–14, 21–17, and 22–14. He then dropped to 14–19 in 1952 in what turned out to be the Braves' last season in Boston. In one game that year, Warren struck out 18 batters in 15 innings and hit a home run but still lost to the Cubs, 2–1.

Nevertheless, Warren had become one of the premier pitchers in a game that at the time was overflowing with outstanding moundsmen. He was not only a magnificent hurler, though. He had a smooth, classic delivery that made his presence unforgettable.

Spahn would start his motion by pumping both arms back. Then, arms raised far above his head, he would rock back, kicking his right leg high into the air before coming back down with a straight overhand motion, releasing the ball from a perfectly balanced position. It was pure poetry, the work of an ultimate craftsman.

"I tried to get all the momentum I could going to the plate," Spahn said. "It [the motion] wasn't for show. It just came normally and was part of my success. And when hitters told me they had trouble with my delivery, I worked even harder on it."

The hurler's hard work continued when the Braves moved to Milwaukee. And it paid off with records of 23–7, 21–12, 17–14, 20–11, 21–11, 22–11, 21–15, 21–10, 21–13, 18–14, and 23–7 from 1953 through 1963. Along the way, Spahn changed from a power pitcher to a finesse hurler, developing a baffling assortment of curves, screwballs, sliders, and changeups that constantly kept opposing hitters off balance.

"He was the best lefty in the business," said Willie Mays. The venerable Branch Rickey called Warren "the consummate artist." "He makes my job easy," said Braves pitching coach and former star hurler Whit Wyatt. "Every pitch he throws has an idea behind it."

Spahn had numerous milestone games during his career. He won the Braves' first game in Milwaukee, a 3–2 decision in 10 innings over the St. Louis Cardinals. Warren won the 1953 All-Star Game at Crosley Field in a 5–1 National League triumph. That year, only a fourth-inning infield hit by Richie Ashburn kept Spahn from hurling a no-hitter in a 5–0 decision over the Philadelphia Phillies.

In 1957, after pitching the Braves to the National League pennant and winning the Cy Young Award, he lost the World Series opener with the New York Yankees, 3–1, but returned to win Game Four, 7–5, in 10 innings in a Fall Classic made noteworthy by the three victories of Warren's roommate Lew Burdette. Another World Series with the Yanks followed in 1958, and this time Spahn won the opener in 10 innings, 4–3, then fired a two-hitter to win Game Four, 3–0, before absorbing a 10-inning loss in the sixth game, 4–3. The Braves lost this Series in seven games.

The brilliant southpaw finally got a no-hitter on September 16, 1960 when, at 39 years old, he blanked the Phillies, 4–0, striking out 15 and walking two. Seven months later, on April 28, 1961, he tossed another no-hitter, this time with a five-strikeout, two-walk, 1–0 verdict over the San Francisco Giants. In his next outing, Spahn tossed a two-hitter to beat the Los Angeles Dodgers, 4–1.

Spahn became the winningest lefthander of all time in 1963 when he defeated the New York Mets on opening day, 6–1, for his 328th career victory. Later that season, the 42-year-old lefty hurled one of his most remarkable games when he matched pitches with the Giants' Juan Marichal for 15 innings before losing, 1–0, on Mays's 16th-inning home run.

After posting a 23–7 record that year, Spahn slipped to 6–13 in 1964. That November, he was sold to the Mets, where he briefly rejoined his original big league manager, Casey Stengel. Warren went 4–12 for a terrible Mets team before drawing his release in August. He was picked up by the Giants and won three of seven games, including a 9–2 victory over the Cubs for the last win of his career.

Released again, the ageless Spahn refused to give in. "I didn't quit; baseball retired me," he said. He then went to Mexico, where he worked in three games in 1967, trying to prove he could still pitch at the age of 45. That didn't work out, and Spahn returned to the United States in 1968 as manager of the Tulsa team in the Pacific Coast League. He pitched a few games for Tulsa before hanging up his glove for good.

Spahn managed at Tulsa for five years, winning the pennant in 1968 and getting named PCL Manager of the Year. Afterward, he put in stints as a scout and minor league pitching coach in the Cardinals organization, pitching coach with the Cleveland Indians, minor league instructor with the California Angels, and special pitching instructor in Japan. He left baseball in 1981 to devote his considerable energies to public relations work and to his 2,800-acre cattle ranch in Oklahoma.

August 11, 1961—Braves 2, Cubs 1

Chicago	AB	R	H	RBI	Milwaukee	AB	R	H	RBI
Heist, cf	4	0	0	0	Cimoli, cf	4	1	2	1
Zimmer, 2b	4	0	2	0	Bolling, 2b	4	0	0	0
Santo, 3b	3	1	0	0	Mathews, 3b	4	0	1	0
Altman, rf	4	0	1	0	Aaron, rf	2	0	1	0
Williams, lf	4	0	1	0	Adcock, 1b	2	0	0	0
Rodgers, 1b	4	0	1	1	Thomas, lf	3	0	1	0
Kindall, ss	4	0	1	0	Torre, c	3	1	0	0
Bertell, c	3	0	0	0	McMillan, ss	3	0	1	0
a–Banks, ph	1	0	0	0	Spahn, p	2	0	0	1
Curtis, p	2	0	0	0					
b–McAnany, ph	1	0	0	0					
Totals	34	1	6	1		27	2	6	2

Chicago	0	0	0	0	0	1	0	0	0	–	1
Milwaukee	0	0	0	0	1	0	0	1	x	–	2

a–Safe on error for Bertell in 9th.
b–Flied out for Curtis in 9th.

Chicago	IP	H	R	ER	BB	SO
Curtis (L)	8	6	2	1	2	6

Milwaukee	IP	H	R	ER	BB	SO
Spahn (W)	9	6	1	1	1	5

DP–Milwaukee 1, Chicago 1. LOB–Chicago 8, Milwaukee 4. E–Williams, Bolling, Mathews. HR–Cimoli. SB–Aaron. SF–Santo. SFF–Spahn. T–2:25. A–40,775.

Early Wynn

Expert in Intimidation

If there was ever a pitcher who carried to the mound a meaner disposition than Early Wynn, he surely wasn't from this planet. When
it came to facing enemy hitters, Wynn was about as nasty as anyone
who ever toed the rubber.

Wynn didn't just dislike opposing batsmen. He detested them.
He called them his mortal enemies. And if one of them just happened to rub Early the wrong way, he would be well advised to have
a doctor waiting nearby.

Gus, a name given to Wynn early in his career by teammate
Ellis Clary because, he said, "he looked like a Gus" (who would
ever call such a tough guy Early?), was one of the lingering rem-
nants of an era when pitchers worked with little regard for the safe-
ty of the hitters they faced. Brushback and even beanball pitches
were standard parts of a moundsman's arsenal, and retaliation was
a common strategic device.

Early Wynn pitched longer than any hurler in American League history.

Wynn was once quoted as saying he'd knock down his own grandmother if she crowded the plate. "I've got the right to knock down anybody holding a bat," he said.

True to his word, Early once knocked down his own son after the kid sprayed a series of line drives off the fence during a batting practice session at Comiskey Park. "What else could I do?" Wynn asked. "He was leaning in on me, and I knocked him on his butt to show him who was the boss.

"The pitching mound is my office," Wynn claimed, adding that he didn't like a messy office. He also said that a pitcher couldn't be a good one unless he "hated the hitters." Of course, intimidation was very much a part of Wynn's game plan.

"There isn't a man in baseball who, if he is not stupid or lying, will not admit that he is afraid of him," New York Yankees manager Casey Stengel said. "He is not polite to hitters. He gives them that stare, and he makes them duck, and he just isn't very friendly."

When he was on the mound, the surly Early wasn't even friendly with friends. The great first baseman Mickey Vernon, a teammate of Wynn's with the Washington Senators and a roommate after the two were traded to the Cleveland Indians, tells a story about his getting four hits off Gus after being swapped back to the Senators. "After the fourth hit, he looked over and yelled, 'Hey roomie, the next time I see you, you're going down,'" Vernon recalled. "Next time we met, he threw one toward my head. 'Just wanted you to know I didn't forget,' he hollered."

Another time, Wynn invited slugger Ted Williams to accompany him on an off-season fishing trip in the Florida Everglades. An avid fisherman, Williams rejected the invitation. "No hitter would go into the Everglades with a pitcher like you," he told Wynn. "His body might never be found."

Wynn was such a fierce competitor and plied his trade with such grim intensity that he once refused to leave the mound after a shot by Jose Valdivielso hit him in the chin. Eventually, manager Al Lopez persuaded him to leave, but only after a prolonged argument. Ultimately, Wynn lost seven teeth and needed 16 stitches to close the wound.

"His expression never changed on the mound," Vernon said. "He always looked mean. He'd get that way before the game and he'd stay that way until it was over. He hated to have anybody bunt on him or hit one up through the middle. If you did that, he'd knock you down the next time up. When he wasn't playing, he always rooted hard for our pitcher and he was a real bench jockey. He'd get down in the corner of the dugout and really let the opposing team have it."

Two contradictions surface. Although he reveled in knocking opposing hitters down, Wynn had sufficient control that he hit only 65 batters in 4,564 innings of major league work. And off the field, Gus was an amiable, cheerful, easy-going guy who loved practical jokes.

Wynn is one of the rare players whose major league career spanned four decades. He pitched 23 seasons in the American League, longer than any other hurler in the junior circuit's history. He made his first appearance in 1939 and his last in 1963. In between, he compiled a 300–244 record with a 3.54 ERA in 691 games. Gus struck out 2,334 and walked 1,775 while allowing 4,291 hits. He registered 49 shutouts and 290 complete games and tossed nine two-hitters.

A burly 6-foot, 200-pound righthander with a slow, deliberate delivery, Wynn was a 20-game winner five times and led the American League in games started five times, in innings pitched three times, in strikeouts and walks each twice, and in ERA once. He was just wild enough to be scary, walking more than 100 batters eight times. A pitcher on seven All-Star teams—and winner of the 1958 contest—he was elected to the Hall of Fame in 1972, attracting votes on 301 of the 396 ballots cast.

Although he had many noteworthy games, including one-hitters in 1955 against the Detroit Tigers and in 1959 against the Boston Red Sox when he struck out 14 and homered and doubled in a 1–0 triumph, Wynn's most celebrated win—yet one of his toughest—was his 300th. It came while he was pitching with the Indians on July 13, 1963, in the second game of a doubleheader against the Royals at Kansas City.

Wynn was obsessed with entering the magic 300 circle, and his quest for that plateau began in earnest in 1961 while he was with the Chicago White Sox. But in early June of that year, he popped a tendon in his right elbow while throwing to first on a fielding play. He pitched only once more the rest of the season, ending up with just eight victories.

Having also suffered gout for many years, Wynn struggled to come back in 1962. With the help of a doctor from Johns Hopkins

Few major league pitchers disliked hitters more than **Early Wynn**.

Hospital in Baltimore, he reported to camp in exceptional shape. But he won only seven games all season (while losing 15). He won his 299th in early September, but two more losses closed out the season.

Released from his contract, Wynn went to spring training in 1963 with the White Sox as a nonroster invitee. Ineffective, the 43-year-old hurler was released as the team broke camp. But he was given a reprieve when signed by Cleveland, a team in desperate need of pitching help.

Wynn made five starts, losing twice, although pitching respectably. Finally the goal he had sought for so long materialized. Working five innings and giving up four runs and six hits, Gus got the decision in a 7–4 victory over the Royals. Two-run singles in the top of the fifth by Joe Adcock and Al Luplow gave the Indians a lead they never relinquished. Jerry Walker pitched the last four innings to preserve the win, after Wynn had yielded a three-run double to Jerry Lumpe in the bottom of the fifth.

"I was exhausted," said Wynn, who admitted he had been awake most of the previous night because "my gout was killing me. Every pitch got to be a great effort. If Birdie Tebbetts [the manager] hadn't gotten me out of there when he did, I might have fallen on my face. But I felt I had this one coming to me. I hope I don't seem to be greedy, but I wanted that one more than anything."

No one could blame him for feeling that way. After all, it was the climax of a long and sparkling career for Wynn that had begun in 1936. That year, dressed in overalls and lugging a battered glove, the 16-year-old farm boy from Hartford, Alabama, where he was born January 6, 1920, attended a tryout camp given by the Washington Senators.

Possessing a crackling fastball but nothing else, Wynn sufficiently impressed Senators camp director Clyde Milan that he was offered a Class D contract paying him $100 a month. Wynn took it and the following year found himself at Sanford in the Florida State League, where he fashioned a 16–11 record. Wynn spent the next two years at Charlotte of the Piedmont League, where he accumulated a 25–25 mark over that period. He was called up by the Senators at the end of the 1939 season and appeared in three games (losing two), the most distinguishing feature being that he bunted into a triple play while trying to lay down a sacrifice. Wynn then spent the next season back at Charlotte and the 1941 campaign at Springfield in the Eastern League before returning to Washington to stay at the end of the season.

Gus spent the next six seasons in Washington, playing with a team that regularly occupied the lower regions of the American League standings. He went 10–16 in his first full season in 1942, but—with one year out for military service, during which he drove a truck transporting high explosives—he was not terribly overwhelming, although he was the lowly Nats' best pitcher. His best records were an 18–12 in 1943 and a 17–15 in 1947.

Wynn caught a big break late in 1948 when he and Vernon were traded to Cleveland for Eddie Robinson and two others. Not only was Gus moving to a team that had just won a World Series, but he was joining forces with one of the game's premier pitching coaches, ex–big league hurler Mel Harder.

Harder taught Wynn there was more to pitching than just unleashing the high fastball that Early loved to throw. Under Harder's tutelage, Gus learned how to throw breaking balls and how to change speeds. Wynn for the first time became a well-rounded pitcher.

It showed. Wynn went 29–15 in his first two seasons with Cleveland, leading the league with a 3.20 ERA in 1950, when he was 18–8. Then in 1951 he became a 20-game winner for the first time with a 20–13 mark. He followed that with a 23–12 record in 1952.

Wynn was now not only one of the league's premier hurlers, but a member of an extraordinary pitching staff. The Indians featured a starting rotation that included future Hall of Famers Wynn, Bob Feller, and Bob Lemon, as well as Mike Garcia. Between 1949 and 1955, the rotation posted a combined record of 443–278, and in 1954, when Cleveland won the pennant with a league record 111 victories, it had—with the help of Hal Newhouser, Art Houtteman, and relievers Ray Narleski and Don Mossi—the lowest staff ERA (2.78) of any American League team since 1919.

"I think," said manager Al Lopez in a masterful understatement some years later, "that we had one of the greatest pitching staffs ever put together."

Wynn, whose 23–11 record during the regular season tied with Lemon for the league lead in victories, dropped his only outing in the '54 World Series—a second-game, 3–1 loss to the New York Giants in a game in which Dusty Rhodes drove in all three runs. But Early would go on to a glorious nine-year stint in Cleveland that included a 20–9 mark in 1956.

Seemingly slowing down in the eyes of trade-happy general manager Frank Lane after a 14–17 mark, Wynn was swapped after the 1957 season to the White Sox in a deal that brought Minnie Minoso to Cleveland. But Gus was far from through.

After becoming the first major league pitcher to lead his league in strikeouts in consecutive years with different teams, despite a 14–16 record, he exploded to 22–10 in 1959 to pace the White Sox to their first pennant in 40 years. At the age of 39, Wynn led the league in wins, was named winner of the Cy Young Award and American League Comeback Player of the Year, and was third in the MVP voting. He capped a brilliant season with a six-hit, 11–0 win over the Los Angeles Dodgers in the World Series opener before getting knocked out early in Game Four and losing the sixth and deciding game, 9–3, following another quick exit.

Wynn, an able hitter who had 17 career home runs, had one more good season with the Chisox when he recorded a 13–12 mark in 1960. By then, his salary had reached its highest level at $45,000. Soon afterward, his pursuit of a 300th win elevated to obsessive levels until Gus's quest was finally rewarded in 1963.

After his 300th victory, Wynn never won another game. He made 15 more appearances in 1963, all but one in relief, before retiring at the end of the season.

The following year, he replaced his old mentor, Mel Harder, as pitching coach with the Indians, a job he held for three years. After that, he served as a coach with the Minnesota Twins, minor league manager, major league scout, and broadcaster with the Twins, Toronto Blue Jays, and White Sox. Wynn returned to his home in Nokomis, Florida, in the early 1980s, where he lived a comfortable life after accumulating a considerable amount of wealth from his investments and as the owner of a heavy construction company. He died in 1999 at the age of 79.

July 13, 1963—Indians 7, Royals 4

Cleveland	AB	R	H	RBI	Kansas City	AB	R	H	RBI
Francona, lf	5	0	1	0	Tartabull, cf	5	1	1	0
Tasby, lf	0	0	0	0	Causey, ss	5	0	0	0
Howser, ss	5	1	2	0	Lumpe, 2b	4	0	1	3
Kirkland, cf	5	2	1	0	Alusik, rf	3	1	1	1
Alvis, 3b	4	1	0	0	Lau, c	3	0	1	0
Adcock, 1b	4	1	1	3	Charles, 3b	2	0	1	0
Romano, c	3	1	2	1	Essegian, lf	4	0	0	0
Luplow, rf	2	0	2	2	Harrelson, 1b	3	1	2	0
Brown, 2b	4	0	1	1	Drabowsky, p	1	0	1	0
Wynn, p	2	1	1	0	Willis, p	0	0	0	0
c–Held, ph	1	0	1	0	a–Cimoli, ph	1	0	1	0
Walker, p	0	0	0	0	b–LaRussa, pr	0	1	0	0
					Fischer, p	0	0	0	0
					d–Siebern, ph	1	0	0	0
					Lovrich, p	0	0	0	0
					e–Edwards, ph	1	0	0	0
Totals	35	7	12	7		33	4	9	4

Cleveland	0	1	0	0	4	0	1	0	1	–	7
Kansas City	0	0	0	1	3	0	0	0	0	–	4

a–Singled for Willis in 5th.
b–Ran for Cimoli in 5th.
c–Doubled for Wynn in 6th.
d–Struck out for Fischer in 6th.
e–Fouled out for Lovrich in 9th.

Cleveland	IP	H	R	ER	BB	SO
Wynn (W)	5	6	4	4	3	3
Walker	4	3	0	0	2	2
Kansas City						
Drabowsky (L)	4⅔	6	5	5	5	5
Willis	⅓	1	0	0	0	0
Fischer	1	2	0	0	0	0
Lovrich	3	3	2	1	1	1

DP–Kansas City 1. LOB–Cleveland 8, Kansas City 7. E–Harrelson. 2B–Lumpe, Held, Lau. 3B–Kirkland. HR–Alusik. SB–Kirkland. SFF–Adcock. T–2:42. A–13,565.

Gaylord Perry

Master of Mind Games

No pitcher in baseball history ever worked under more scrutiny than Gaylord Perry. The big righthander never took the mound without dozens of eyes focusing on every move he made.

When Perry pitched, he was watched with the kind of intensity a spy would command in the Pentagon. It was as though every opponent, umpire, sportswriter, and a lot of fans had been commissioned by the FBI. And many brought their binoculars, cameras, and test kits to help record their observations.

Such rigorous surveillance, of course, had a readily available explanation. Throughout his career, Perry was accused of using illegal substances on the baseballs he threw. The watchdogs were trying to catch him in the act.

It was charged that Perry threw a spitball, a pitch that baseball had outlawed long ago in 1920. It was claimed that in addition to saliva he used all manner of other substances to doctor a baseball.

At 40 years of age, **Gaylord Perry** was the oldest pitcher to win the Cy Young Award.

Vaseline, baby oil, slippery elm, and files were among the ones most often mentioned. He would, they said, hide the substance under his hat, behind his ears, in his pocket, in his glove, on his neck, or in his uniform.

With a chuckle, Gaylord would deny it. "I always liked the hitter to believe that I was throwing a doctored ball," he said. "I couldn't say I never threw one because then the hitters might believe me." Actually, Perry claimed, the balls that he hurled that took such a precipitous dive when they reached the plate were really his hard slider or sometimes a forkball.

Few believed him. Teams would often stop games to have balls checked. Umpires constantly inspected balls Perry had thrown and repeatedly trekked to the mound to check for a hidden substance. Once, the Boston Red Sox sent several balls Gaylord had thrown to a lab to check for foreign material. Another time, the New York Yankees focused two cameras on him for the entire game, trying to spot Perry loading up.

Perry finally confirmed his opponents' suspicions in 1974 when he wrote in his autobiography, *Me and the Spitter,* that he did indeed load up his pitches. But he said he had stopped doing it. Although no one believed that, either, he was never caught until late in his career when during a game in 1982 Perry was ejected for doctoring a ball and ultimately fined and suspended.

Throughout his career, Perry delighted in confounding the sentinels who watched him. Before each pitch, he performed a series of rituals, fidgeting, pulling on his cap, yanking on his uniform, rubbing his glove, gyrating his shoulders. It was all designed to throw the hitters off balance and to give them an illusion that may or may not have been true.

Perry was a master at playing mind games with the hitters. He figured that the more he could make them think, the more confused they'd get and the more effective he'd be. "I'd like to lead the league each year in psych-outs," he once said.

Without question, he did that. But he was also one of the best in a variety of pitching categories, too. During a 22-year career in which he played for eight teams, Gaylord fashioned a 314–265 record, three times topping the league in wins, and twice leading in complete games and innings pitched.

Although he rarely played with a contender and never in a World Series, Gaylord was a workhorse. His 5,350.1 innings pitched ranks sixth highest in baseball, and his 690 games started places seventh on the all-time list. He worked more than 200 innings in 17 different seasons, and five times he went over 300.

Overall, Perry appeared in 777 games. He completed 303 of his starts, 53 of them being shutouts. His career earned run average was

3.11, and he struck out 3,534, walked 1,379, and gave up 4,938 hits—the fourth highest total in baseball.

A 20-game winner five times and a winner in double figures 17 times, Perry was the first pitcher to capture the Cy Young Award in both leagues and just one of four hurlers to win 100 games in each circuit. He has a no-hitter to his credit. And with his older brother Jim (a Cy Young winner in 1970), the Perrys have more combined wins (529) than any brothers except the Niekros.

Gaylord, who was elected to the Hall of Fame in 1991, collecting 342 votes of the 443 cast, won his 300th game May 6, 1982, when he hurled the Seattle Mariners to a 7–3 victory over the Yankees at the Kingdome. Perry was 43 at the time, baseball's oldest active player. They called him "The Ancient Mariner."

Released at the end of the previous season by the Atlanta Braves when he was just three short of his 300th win, Perry joined Seattle in 1982 after the Mariners were the only team to offer him a contract. He beat the Yankees for his 299th win on April 30, then beat them again to become the first pitcher since 1963 to reach 300 victories. Gaylord struck out four while yielding nine hits. The Mariners put the win away with five runs (four unearned due to a two-base throwing error by New York catcher Rick Cerone) in the third inning, the key hits being run-scoring singles by Terry Bulling and Manny Castillo, a two-run single by Todd Cruz, and an RBI triple by Al Cowens.

"It took a long time to get, but I finally put it together," said Perry, who changed uniform shirts after each inning and later sold them on the memorabilia market. "I worked 20 years for this. When I started out, I never thought I'd get to 300 wins. But they just kept piling up. The thing that helped me get there was staying healthy. I never had a serious injury in my career."

Perry's victory total had been launched way back in 1962 when he broke in with the San Francisco Giants. He had spent four years in the minors before getting there, and even more years toiling as a youth on the sandlots of North Carolina, hoping someday to become a major leaguer.

Gaylord Perry wipes off perspiration, something he was accused of putting on baseballs.

Gaylord was born September 15, 1938, in Williamston, North Carolina, the son of a poor tenant farmer. Evan Perry didn't have much money, but he knew baseball, having been a prominent semi-pro pitcher for many years. He not only taught his sons the game, but also did their farm chores on days when they had ball games.

The first uniforms worn by the Perry boys were made out of fertilizer sacks sewed together by their mother. That hardly fazed them. Both became local sensations, with Gaylord playing third base when Jim, who was two years older, pitched.

"Jim pitched twice a week, and that was all the pitching we needed," Gaylord said. "But one year we went to the playoffs, and we were playing three–four games a week and needed another pitcher. That's how I got started."

Gaylord found that the mound suited him perfectly. Ultimately, he tossed five no-hitters for his high school team and didn't allow a single earned run in his senior year.

After briefly attending Campbell College, Perry signed with the Giants, getting a $90,000 bonus. He had only modest success in his first three years in the minors, winning just 28 games and losing 29 during stops at St. Cloud, Corpus Christi, and Rio Grande Valley.

"When that boy starts to throw the ball the way he was built to throw it," said Giants farm director and Hall of Fame pitcher Carl Hubbell, "he'll be a big winner."

Perry soon proved Hubbell right. In 1961, playing for Tacoma in the Pacific Coast League, the 6-foot, 4-inch, 215-pound hurler began to live up to his potential with a 16–10 record that earned him the league's Pitcher of the Year honors. That got him a promotion to the Giants the following year. But Gaylord's big league stay was short lived. After appearing in 13 games, he was sent back to Tacoma. The same scenario was repeated in 1963.

Gaylord finally made the big leagues to stay in 1964. Although he hurled 10 scoreless innings of relief to get the decision in an 8–6 win over the New York Mets in a 23-inning, seven-hour, 22-minute second game of a doubleheader, he was mostly mediocre, going 20–23 over the next two seasons while pitching as much in relief as he did as a starter. In 1966, however, Perry became the special project of Giants pitching coach Larry Jansen, a former mound standout with the New York Giants. His career would be changed forever.

"He taught me to throw a hard slider," Perry said. "That's what made the difference. From that point on, I became a winning pitcher."

Some said that the pitch Perry learned to throw was a spitball. Regardless, that season, Perry was the hottest pitcher in baseball. He had a 20–2 record by late August. In one game, he had a no-hitter into the eighth inning, eventually striking out 15 in a 4–1 win over the Philadelphia Phillies. He appeared in his first of five All-Star Games, and was the winning pitcher in the National League's 2–1, 10-inning victory. A September slump cooled him off, but he still finished with a 21–8 mark.

Perry slipped to 15–17 in 1967, but that wasn't entirely his fault. He lost nine one-run games. Once, he hurled 16 shutout innings before the Giants won, 1–0, in the 21st. The following year, his record was 16–15, which included a no-hit game against the St. Louis Cardinals and Bob Gibson. Gaylord struck out nine and walked two, winning 1–0 on Ron Hunt's first-inning home run. Incredibly, the Cardinals' Ray Washburn pitched a no-hitter against the Giants the very next day.

Over the next three years, Perry won 58 games while losing 39. He won 19 in 1969, then posted a 23–13 mark the following year while leading the league in wins and games started, and for the second straight year in innings pitched, with 328.2. After the 1971 season, however, the Giants traded Gaylord to the Cleveland Indians in a deal that brought Sam McDowell to San Francisco.

Gaylord was an instant hit in Cleveland. He posted a 24–16 mark in 1972 with a career-low 1.92 ERA and a league-leading 29 complete games for the fifth-place Indians. He then won his first Cy Young Award.

Perry followed that with 19–19 and 21–13 seasons for the lowly Indians. In 1973, a year in which he set a career high with 238 strikeouts, Gaylord lost a 5–4 decision to his brother Jim, then with the Detroit Tigers, in the first American League game in which brothers started against each other. Gaylord won 15 games in a row in 1974.

Between 1969 and 1975, Perry worked in more than 300 innings in six of the seven years. Gaylord, who in the off-season always returned to North Carolina to work on the farm, prided himself on his strength and durability. He never had a sore arm, and the only time he ever spent on the disabled list was for an ankle injury.

"My arm was always strong," he said. "I guess that was because I always did a lot of physical work on the farm. That, plus the fact that I always kept in shape. Every year, I started a workout program on January 1, and I would be ready to go by spring training."

Perry was also a fierce competitor. He hated to lose, and he would glare with fire in his eyes at teammates who made mistakes behind him. And he was not opposed to evaluating the performances of his managers, especially when he thought their strategy deserved to be questioned.

After winning 70 games at Cleveland in three and one-half years, Perry was traded to the Texas Rangers. That began a nomadic existence during which, over an eight-year period leading up to the end of his career, Gaylord would also play with the San Diego Padres, Rangers again, Yankees, Braves, Mariners, and finally the Kansas City Royals, never spending much time in any one place.

His best year during that period came in 1978 when he posted a sparkling 21–6 record with the Padres. That earned him his second Cy Young Award. At 40 years old, he was the oldest player to claim the honor.

Perry was now getting closer to the ultra-special 300-win level, and he pursued that milestone with single-minded purpose. Along the way, he became only the third pitcher in major league history to record 3,000 strikeouts. Finally, he reached 300 during a 10–12 season in Seattle.

The following year, Perry split his time between Seattle and Kansas City before retiring at the end of the season. It was his 22d year in the major leagues. "The only secret to longevity," Gaylord said, "is you have to take care of your body."

Perry became a full-time farmer, growing soybeans, peanuts, and corn. After a while, the farm went bankrupt. Gaylord then dabbled in the insurance business, coached baseball at Campbell College, and sold memorabilia, much of it his own. And years after he had stopped playing, he was still being asked if he threw a spitter.

May 6, 1982—Mariners 7, Yankees 3

New York	AB	R	H	RBI	Seattle	AB	R	H	RBI
Randolph, 2b	5	1	1	0	J. Cruz, 2b	3	1	0	0
Griffey, rf	4	2	3	1	Castillo, 3b	4	2	2	2
Mumphrey, cf	4	0	2	0	Bochte, lf	4	0	2	1
Mayberry, 1b	4	0	0	0	Zisk, dh	4	0	1	0
Winfield, lf	4	0	1	1	T. Cruz, ss	4	1	2	2
Gamble, dh	4	0	1	1	Cowens, rf	4	0	1	1
Smalley, 3b	3	0	1	0	Simpson, cf	4	0	0	0
Cerone, c	4	0	0	0	Maler, 1b	3	1	1	0
Dent, ss	2	0	0	0	Bulling, c	3	2	2	1
Murcer, ph	1	0	0	0					
Milbourne, ss	1	0	0	0					
Totals	36	3	9	3		33	7	11	7

New York	0	0	0	0	0	1	0	2	0	–	3
Seattle	0	0	5	0	0	0	2	0	x	–	7

New York	IP	H	R	ER	BB	SO
Alexander (L)	3	6	5	1	0	2
May	5	5	2	2	0	2
Seattle						
Perry (W)	9	9	3	3	1	4

DP–New York 1, Seattle 1. LOB–New York 7, Seattle 3. E–Castillo, Cerone. 2B–Bochte, Zisk, Bulling, Castillo. 3B–Mumphrey, Maler, Cowens. HR–Griffey. SH–J. Cruz. WP–May. T–2:29. A–27,369.

Steve Carlton

No Distractions Allowed

Among the many players who have hurled baseballs for a living, it's unlikely that any pitcher ever dominated hitters more than Steve Carlton.

When Carlton was on the mound, the chances of a hitter connecting with one of his deliveries were slim to none. With an overpowering fastball and a devastating slider, Carlton, when he was right—and he usually was—simply overmatched most hitters, routinely sending them back to the dugout cursing their misfortune.

"Hitting him," said Pittsburgh Pirates Hall of Fame slugger Willie Stargell, "was like trying to drink coffee with a fork."

Although the slender lefthander's bread and butter pitches during the prime of his career with the Philadelphia Phillies were his fastball and slider, he also had an exceptional changeup and a nasty curve. He had pinpoint control, and he was as strong and as durable as a Baldwin locomotive.

In one amazing season, **Steve Carlton** won 27 of the Phillies' 59 victories.

Quite possibly no player ever devoted more time and energy to his own physical condition than Carlton. A day never passed when he didn't work out. And his workouts consisted of strenuous tests that mere mortals would never attempt. Often, they'd last for six hours, sometimes extending into the wee hours of the morning—after he'd pitched a game.

One of his special workouts was walking back and forth countless times in a 4-by-12-foot box in 3-foot-deep rice. He also did

1,100 sit-ups at a time with 15-pound weights strapped to each wrist and each ankle. Even on days when he pitched, he performed stretching exercises for one and one-half hours before the game. These and his other super-human drills kept Carlton in marvelous shape, even when he was well past the age of 40.

"He's not only one of the greatest athletes I ever worked with," said former Phillies strength and conditioning coach Gus Hoefling, who with Steve devised the pitcher's fanatical fitness regimen. "He's the best conditioned. Whoever put that man together genetically did one helluva job."

Carlton's mental strength matched the power of his body. He was totally focused on his work, having the ability to shut out distractions, concentrate fully on pitching, and emphasize a strong positive approach. Before games, Carlton would almost go into a trance as he prepared himself for the battle ahead.

"The mental part of my game was the most important part of my approach," he once said. "I knew what I needed to do to succeed. My job was my performance on the field, so whatever was an intangible or an outside influence that was not necessary, I found a way to eliminate it."

One particular element that Carlton eliminated with a considerable degree of notoriety was the media. Because of what he considered inaccurate and unfair reporting, he stopped talking to the press a few years after arriving in Philadelphia. Thereafter, he steadfastly refused to give interviews for the rest of his playing career.

Carlton's silence only added to his mystique. Although amiable and even charming in private, he was a recluse as far as his public persona was concerned. Viewed as eccentric, his perceived stoicism forbade all but a few outsiders from entering his inner world, in the process canceling any possibility of his sharing his insights and particular pitching philosophy with anyone but his closest confidants.

It was a world that had many parts, none larger, though, than what Carlton accomplished when he fired baseballs at opposing batters.

Steve Carlton signs a contract negotiated by Phillies general manager Paul Owens.

During a major league career that reached from 1965 to 1988, the 6-foot, 4-inch, 210-pound southpaw posted a 329–244 record while working in 741 games. In 5,217.1 innings, he gave up 4,672 hits, struck out 4,136, and walked 1,833 while completing 254 of the 709 games he started, including 55 shutouts. His career earned run average was 3.22.

Carlton ranks second in baseball history in strikeouts and walks, fifth in games started, and ninth in innings pitched. He has more strikeouts than any lefthander and trails only Warren Spahn among southpaws in wins. He also started 14 opening-day games, a figure exceeded only by Tom Seaver

"Lefty," as he's called by his friends, was a 20-game winner six times. He won in double figures 18 years in a row. Carlton is just one of three pitchers ever to have won four Cy Young Awards. He is the owner of six one-hitters. He struck out 19 in a single game,

16 in each of two other games, and fanned the side an amazing 124 times during his career. He led the league in strikeouts and innings pitched, each five times, and in wins four. Twelve times he pitched in more than 250 innings in a season. He was chosen for 10 All-Star teams, working in five of the games and getting the win in 1969. And he holds the National League records for most consecutive starting assignments (534) and most starts (677).

A fine batter whose 346 hits rank seventh on the all-time list, Carlton was elected to the Hall of Fame in 1994, garnering 436 votes of 455 ballots cast (95.82 percent).

"Lefty was a craftsman, an artist," another Hall of Famer, former player and longtime Phillies broadcaster Richie Ashburn, once said. "He was a perfectionist. He painted a ballgame. Stroke, stroke, stroke, and when he got through it was a masterpiece. There was nothing accidental about it. His games were perfectly orchestrated."

Right from the time he signed his first pro contract, it was obvious that Carlton, who was born December 22, 1944, in Miami, Florida, was destined to be someone special. Given a $5,000 bonus by the St. Louis Cardinals in 1964, the 19-year-old youngster made an immediate impact when he fashioned a 10–1 record, allowing just 39 hits in 79 innings and striking out 91 for Rock Hill in the Western Carolina League. Too good for that league, Carlton was moved up to Winnipeg, then to Double-A Tulsa before his first pro season was over.

Although he pitched in only 15 games with no decisions, Carlton spent the entire 1965 season with the Cardinals before going back to Tulsa the following year. At mid-season, the Cardinals summoned the young southpaw to Cooperstown to pitch in the annual Hall of Fame game against the Minnesota Twins. Steve struck out 10 Twins, and soon thereafter he was in the big leagues to stay. He won his first game August 5, 1966, beating the New York Mets, 7–1.

As a full-fledged member of the Cardinals' starting rotation, Carlton went 14–9 in 1967, even drawing a starting assignment in the fifth game of the World Series against the Detroit Tigers, which he lost, 3–1. Over the next three years, while pitching twice in relief in the 1968 World Series, Carlton won 40 games, the most notable victory being a 1969 outing when he set a major league record for a nine-inning game (since tied) by striking out 19 Mets in a contest that he incredibly lost, 4–3.

If he wasn't there already, Carlton assured himself a place among the elite hurlers of the National League in 1971 when he finished the season with a 20–9 record. But all was not perfect in St. Louis. Steve wanted a $10,000 raise (to $65,000), but that was more than the Cards were willing to pay. When the dispute between the two parties could not be resolved, St. Louis decided to trade him.

The Cardinals found a willing taker in the Phillies, who were having a similar contract skirmish with their ace pitcher Rick Wise. A trade was arranged, with the two pitchers switching clubs in what turned out to be the last swap for Phillies general manager John Quinn.

Phillies fans were livid. Wise was coming off a 17-win season which included a no-hitter, and he was one of the most popular Philadelphia players. Scores of unhappy fans bombarded the club's switchboard with irate calls, and newspaper articles criticized the Phils for trading away a local favorite.

Carlton, however, soon tamed the angry masses. His first season with the Phillies was one of the best any big league pitcher ever had. While the club was winning just 59 games and finishing deep in last place, Carlton won 27 games, including at one point 15 in a row, while compiling a glittering ERA of 1.97 and striking out 310. He completed 30 of his 41 starts, eight of which resulted in shutouts, worked in a career-high 346.1 innings, and at the end of the season walked away with his first Cy Young Award.

The trade turned out to be the best the Phillies ever made. Although he slumped and lost 20 games in 1973, Carlton was the mainstay of the club's pitching staff for the next 12 years. He won 20 games in 1976, 23 in 1977, 24 in 1980, and 23 in 1982, while helping to drive the Phillies to their best era in club history when they won five division titles, two pennants, and one World Series between 1976 and 1983.

"Coming to Philadelphia was a blessing in disguise," Carlton said. "The turning point of my career was going there. I didn't know what professional baseball could be until then."

Overall, Carlton won four divisional playoff games, beating the Los Angeles Dodgers, 9–4, in the third game in 1978, the Houston Astros, 3–1, in the first game in 1980, and the Dodgers, 1–0, in Game One and 7–2 in the fourth and final game in 1983. He also lost four playoff games, including two to the Montreal Expos in a special playoff in 1981.

Carlton won the second game of the 1980 World Series against the Kansas City Royals, 6–4, then hurled the Phillies to the clincher in a 4–1 verdict in Game Six when the club won its only Series in franchise history. He was on the losing end of a 3–2 decision in the third game of the 1983 Series against the Baltimore Orioles.

Steve won his other Cy Young Awards in 1977, 1980, and 1982. Without question, he was the premier pitcher of his era in the National League.

If there was one weapon in Carlton's many-faceted arsenal that glistened especially brightly, it was his devastating slider. Dropping like a dish falling off a table, it was virtually impossible to hit and formed a perfect complement to Steve's 90-mile-per-hour fastball.

"He could put it at just the right spot at varying speeds and with consistency," said the Los Angeles Dodgers' Steve Garvey. "You'd just hope some days he'd be a little up or down or not able to control it as well, and then maybe you'd get lucky and get a hit."

Through much of the 1970s, Carlton insisted on pitching to one catcher, the veteran Tim McCarver. Although others would catch Lefty after McCarver retired, the two formed an inseparable union that included the talkative backstop's serving as the hurler's chief spokesman.

"When Steve Carlton and I die," McCarver once quipped, "we're going to be buried 60 feet, 6 inches apart."

At the age of 38, Carlton won his 300th game on September 23, 1983, when, pitching in the city where he still lived, he beat his old team, the Cardinals, 6–2, at Busch Stadium. "Warming up, he didn't have very good stuff," said pitching coach Claude Osteen. But Carlton worked eight innings and allowed seven hits, while striking out 12 and walking one for his 15th and final triumph of the season. The Phillies backed Carlton, who drove in the first run with a single, with a 17-hit attack that featured three hits apiece by Mike Schmidt and Gary Matthews. The Cards' runs came in the fourth inning on a two-run homer by David Green.

The win was the eighth in a row and 15th in their last 18 games for the Phillies, who at the time had a three-game lead over the Pittsburgh Pirates in the NL East and were headed for a division title and the National League pennant before losing in five games in the World Series to the Orioles.

Three years later, Carlton reached another milestone when he recorded his 4,000th strikeout, against the Cincinnati Reds Eric Davis. The 1986 season would be Lefty's last in Philadelphia. Released during the season, he then began a sluggish journey in which he won just 11 games while pitching for the San Francisco Giants, Chicago White Sox, Cleveland Indians, and Minnesota Twins before drawing his release at the age of 43 early in the 1988 season. Carlton was reluctant to give up, even trying a brief comeback in spring training the following year with the Phillies, but he eventually realized his career was over. What a magnificent career it had been.

September 23, 1983—Phillies 6, Cardinals 2

Philadelphia	AB	R	H	RBI	St. Louis	AB	R	H	RBI
Morgan, 2b	4	1	1	0	L. Smith, lf	4	0	0	0
Garcia, 2b	1	0	1	0	O. Smith, ss	3	0	1	0
Matuszek, 1b	5	0	2	0	McGee, cf	4	0	1	0
Schmidt, 3b	5	2	3	1	Hendrick, 1b	4	1	1	0
Lefebvre, rf	5	1	2	0	Green, rf	4	1	2	2
Matthews, lf	5	2	3	1	Sexton, 3b	4	0	0	0
Holland, p	0	0	0	0	Lyons, 2b	4	0	0	0
G. Gross, cf, lf	3	0	2	1	Brummer, c	4	0	3	0
Diaz, c	4	0	1	2	Andujar, p	1	0	0	0
DeJesus, ss	4	0	1	0	Lahti, p	0	0	0	0
Carlton, p	4	0	1	1	a-Reyford, ph	1	0	0	0
Dernier, cf	0	0	0	0	Von Ohlen, p	0	0	0	0
					b-Oberkfell, ph	1	0	0	0
Totals	40	6	17	6		34	2	8	2

Philadelphia	0	1	1	0	3	1	0	0	0	– 6
St. Louis	0	0	0	2	0	0	0	0	0	– 2

a–Flied out for Lahti in 7th.
b–Struck out for Von Ohlen in 9th.

Philadelphia	IP	H	R	ER	BB	SO
Carlton (W)	8	7	2	2	1	12
Holland	1	1	0	0	0	2
St. Louis						
Andujar (L)	4⅓	11	5	5	1	3
Lahti	2⅔	4	1	1	0	1
Von Ohlen	2	2	0	0	0	0

DP–St. Louis 3. LOB–Philadelphia 8, St. Louis 7. 2B–Matthews, Morgan, Schmidt.
3B–O. Smith. HR–Green. SB–Schmidt, Lefebvre. S–Andujar. PB–Brummer. T–2:31.
A–27,266.

Tom Seaver

Artist on the Mound

Nothing is more important to a successful pitcher than having a strong arm. There is no such thing as a good hurler with a weak arm.

But there's more to pitching than throwing, and the great moundsmen over the years have all possessed other qualities that made them successful. They have, for instance, in most cases had good brains. Maybe they weren't all quite up to the level of rocket scientists, but at least the great pitchers were usually endowed with a reasonably high degree of innate intelligence.

Tom Seaver is a classic example of the species. He had a good arm. And among his many other attributes, he also had a good head resting atop his strong shoulders. In fact, Seaver no doubt ranks among the smartest hurlers ever to trudge to the top of a pitching mound.

Seaver was a thinking pitcher. Analytical. Shrewd. Always looking for the advantage. Always trying to outsmart the hitters. To use

Tom Seaver holds a record with nine straight seasons of 200 or more strikeouts.

a popular cliché, he pitched with a purpose. "He always knows what he's doing out there," the equally crafty Pete Rose once said.

A powerful 6-foot, 1-inch, 195-pounder, Seaver treated pitching the same way an artist paints a picture. It was an activity that he performed with the utmost care and thought, never leaving anything to chance. "I feel I'm creating something," he said of his mound duties.

What he created mostly was frustration among opposing hitters. With a blazing fastball, his primary pitch, and a wicked slider that handcuffed righthanded batters, Seaver was a master at moving his deliveries up and down and in and out. "I never aim down the middle," he said. "One side or the other, that's all." Rare was the pitch that cut the heart of the plate or that was delivered anywhere near the hitter's preferred zone.

Control played a major role in Seaver's strategy. He could fire a pitch in precisely the place he intended. Sometimes, one pitch would be 2 or 3 inches inside or outside the last one. And he thrived on setting up hitters. "The inside fastball is the pitch that will establish the outside corner for you," he said in Kevin Kerrane's fine book, *The Hurlers.*

Seaver delivered his pitches with a smooth, easy motion reminiscent of his boyhood idol, Hall of Famer Robin Roberts. There was no wasted effort in Seaver's fluid windup. His mechanics were perfect, and when he neared his release, his legs would push off and drive him powerfully toward the plate, his right knee ultimately scraping the dirt in a classic follow-through. Tom was noted for the dirt mark he always carried on the knee of his uniform.

That was about the only spot on Seaver's squeaky-clean image. Sophisticated, articulate, clean-cut, and handsome, he resembled the all-American boy. He had a beautiful wife, Nancy. His father, Charles, played on a Walker Cup golf team in the 1930s. Seaver was fond of art, theater, and the opera, and in his spare time he read and did crossword puzzles. As a rookie, teammates nicknamed him Spanky MacFarland because of his resemblance to the *Our Gang* hero. Later, the press began referring to him as Tom Terrific.

Seaver often mentioned art in his discussions about pitching. "I would like to be a great artist," he once told Dick Schaap. "I would quit pitching if I could paint like Monet or Rousseau. But I can't. What I can do is pitch, and I can do that very well."

He did it so well, in fact, that it landed him in the Hall of Fame in 1992. With 425 votes on the 430 ballots cast, Seaver accumulated the highest percentage of votes (98.84) ever cast for a Hall of Fame inductee.

Tom's career certainly merited such attention. During 20 years in the big leagues, he rang up a 311–205 record with a 2.86 earned run average. He is fourth on the all-time list in strikeouts with 3,640, and tied for seventh in shutouts with 61. He has more opening-day starts (16) than any other hurler and more strikeouts (3,272) than any National League righthander. Seaver pitched in 656 games, starting 647 and completing 231. In 4,782.2 innings, he gave up 3,971 hits and walked just 1,390.

A three-time Cy Young Award winner and member of 12 All-Star teams, he won 20 or more games five times. He hurled one no-hitter and five one-hitters. Seaver holds the major league record for most consecutive seasons (nine) with 200 or more strikeouts. He has a 19-strikeout game to his credit. He led his league in strike-outs five times, while also finishing first in winning percentage four times, in wins and ERA each three times, and in shutouts twice. Always a workhorse, Tom had 16 seasons in which he worked in more than 200 innings, including 13 in a row. He made more than 30 starts 13 straight years and had 16 overall.

Seaver's best work was performed with the New York Mets, a team he led to National League pennants in 1969 and 1973. He is the Mets' all-time leader in virtually every major pitching category. Ironically, two of the biggest games in Seaver's career came when he was wearing the uniforms of the Cincinnati Reds (his no-hitter) and the Chicago White Sox (his 300th win).

Whose uniform Seaver would wear was a major issue at the beginning of his professional career. A native of Fresno, California—born there November 17, 1944—Tom spent two years in the U.S. Marines and some time at Fresno State College before enrolling at the University of Southern California, where scouts soon flocked to watch him pitch. The Los Angeles Dodgers draft-ed Seaver in the 22d round in 1965, but he decided to stay in school. The following year, however, when the Atlanta Braves dan-gled a $40,000 bonus in front of Tom, a free agent, he relented. But baseball commissioner William Eckert voided the contract because Seaver signed after his college season had started, a viola-tion of a major league rule.

Eckert made the Braves ineligible but decreed that any team still interested in Seaver—and willing to match Atlanta's offer—could enter a lottery designed to determine the winner of the 21-year-old hurler's services. With only the Mets, Philadelphia Phillies, and Cleveland Indians interested, sealed bids from each team were placed in a hat and on April 3, 1966, Eckert drew the winning name. It was the Mets.

Pitching was to **Tom Seaver** like painting is to a fine artist.

Seaver was given a $50,000 bonus and assigned to Jacksonville, Florida, in the International League. And in his only season in the minors, Tom posted a 12–12 record while striking out 188 batters in 210 innings.

Moving up to the Mets in 1967, Seaver went 16–13 for a team that lost 101 games and finished in 10th place, 40½ games out of first. Tom was named National League Rookie of the Year. He would win in double figures 15 straight times and 17 overall.

The Mets were slightly better in 1968, and they now had a potentially brilliant young pitching staff featuring Seaver and rookies Nolan Ryan and Jerry Koosman. Seaver won 16 games again and had his first 200-strikeout season. But neither he nor anyone else could have predicted what lay just ahead.

The 1969 Mets were not called "The Miracle Mets" because of some frivolous notion. Catapulting from ninth place the year before, they won the National League pennant in the most improbable fashion, roaring past the front-running Chicago Cubs in mid-September, then, in the year of the first League Championship Series, crushing the Braves in a three-game sweep. A memorable season concluded with New York blitzing the Baltimore Orioles in five games in the World Series.

It was a phenomenal season for Seaver. In helping to transform a laughable team into one of the most revered squads that ever graced the diamonds of New York, he led the Mets with a magnificent 25–7 record during the regular season to earn his first Cy Young Award. He beat the Braves, 9–5, in the first game of the LCS. Then, after losing the World Series opener, 4–1, he came back to capture a 2–1, 10-inning verdict with a complete game six-hitter in Game Four.

Seaver's magnificent pitching continued in 1970. On April 22, he struck out 19 batters in a two-hit, 2–1 win over the San Diego Padres. That not only tied a record at the time, but in fanning the final 10 hitters in a row, Tom set a standard unequaled either before or since. It was also his 13th straight win and paved the way for an 18–12 season.

Tom registered a 20–10 mark in 1971 while leading the league for the second year in a row in both ERA (1.76) and strikeouts with a career-high 289. He then went 21–12 and 19–10, leading the Mets to another National League pennant, with the latter in 1973. That year, while leading the league in ERA, complete games, and strikeouts, Seaver won another Cy Young Award.

He struck out 13 and had a 1–0 lead in the eighth inning but lost the LCS opener, 2–1, to the Cincinnati Reds on home runs by Rose and Johnny Bench. But he was victorious in the deciding fifth game, 7–2, allowing seven hits in eight and one-third innings. In a seven-game World Series won by the Oakland Athletics, Seaver was not involved in the decision after striking out 12 in eight innings in an 11-inning, 3–2 Mets defeat in Game Three. He took the loss in the sixth game, 3–1, after serving a pair of RBI doubles to Reggie Jackson.

Seaver spent three more seasons with the Mets, winning his third Cy Young Award in 1975 after posting a 22–9 record while grabbing his fourth strikeout title. But Tom, who was never able to hide his obsession for winning, was starting to squabble with Mets management. In 1976, the club tried to trade him to the Dodgers for Don Sutton, but the deal was never made after Mets fans raised a ferocious ruckus when the press leaked news of the intended swap.

After a contract dispute that resulted in Seaver's asking to be traded, the Mets finally did swap him in mid-1977 in an eight-player deal with the Reds. Tom pitched five and one-half years in Cincinnati. He finished the '77 campaign with a 21–6 record, then won 56 games over the next four years, including a league-leading 14–2 in the strike-shortened season of 1981.

One of Seaver's most memorable games occurred with the Reds. It happened on June 16, 1978, when Tom, having previously had three no-hit bids broken up in the ninth inning, held the St. Louis Cardinals hitless. En route to a 4–0 victory, he struck out three and walked three.

Injuries curtailed Seaver's efforts in 1982. That winter, he was traded back to the Mets, who by then had sunk to a spot among the doormats of the National League. The 38-year-old hurler went 9–14 for a last-place team. But his stay in New York ended quickly. After the season, the Mets failed to place Seaver on their protected list, and he was drafted by the White Sox.

Contrary to the Mets' thinking, Seaver still had a lot left. He won 31 games over the next two years. In one noteworthy outing in which the White Sox beat the Milwaukee Brewers, 7–6, he was the winner after pitching the last frame of a 25-inning marathon that was resumed the second day after being suspended the night before after 17 innings. He then won the regularly scheduled game, 5–4.

Another major victory occurred on August 4, 1985, when Seaver captured his 300th career win. Ironically, he did it in New

York with a six-hit, 4–1 victory over the Yankees on Phil Rizzuto Day. It was Tom's first attempt at reaching the magic 300 level and came just five days after he'd won his 299th game with a 7–5 victory over the Boston Red Sox.

The 40-year-old Seaver struck out seven and walked one while throwing 145 pitches. At one point, he retired 12 of 13 batters. The White Sox wrapped up the victory with a four-run sixth that featured Bryan Little's two-run single. When the game was over, the huge crowd erupted into a prolonged standing ovation as Tom rushed to the stands to hug his wife.

"It was like I was levitating on the mound," Seaver said. "I hadn't felt like that since 1969 when I was going for a perfect game against the Cubs. This was a constant emotional drain. I'm glad it's over."

The White Sox traded Seaver to the Red Sox midway through the 1986 season. Unfortunately, a knee injury kept Tom out of Boston's meeting with the Mets in the World Series. He became a free agent that winter, and the following season the Mets asked him to try a comeback. After several weeks, Seaver abandoned the attempt, electing instead to retire at the age of 42.

Seaver, however, continued his association with baseball. A communications major in college, he had started doing some broadcasting in 1975 in New York. He continued as a color man on network television during the post-season, and then from 1989 to 1993 served as a television broadcaster for Yankees games. In 1999, he returned to the Mets as a TV announcer and front office executive, handling marketing and community outreach projects and serving as a special pitching instructor.

August 4, 1985—White Sox 4, Yankees 1

Chicago	AB	R	H	RBI	New York	AB	R	H	RBI
Law, lf	3	0	2	0	Henderson, cf	4	0	0	0
Nichols, lf	1	0	1	0	Griffey, dh	4	0	1	1
Little, 2b	2	0	1	2	Mattingly, 1b	4	0	2	0
Fletcher, 2b	1	0	0	0	Winfield, rf	4	0	0	0
Baines, rf	5	0	2	0	Pasqua, lf	4	0	1	0
Walker, 1b	3	0	1	0	Hassey, c	4	0	0	0
Fisk, c	5	1	1	0	Randolph, 2b	3	0	0	0
Gamble, dh	2	1	1	0	Pagliarulo, 3b	3	1	1	0
Kittle, ph	1	0	0	0	Meacham, ss	3	0	1	0
Hulett, 3b	4	1	2	1	a–Baylor, ph	1	0	0	0
Guillen, ss	4	0	1	1					
Salazar, cf	4	1	1	0					
Totals	35	4	13	4		34	1	6	1

| Chicago | 0 | 0 | 0 | 0 | 0 | 4 | 0 | 0 | 0 | – | 4 |
| **New York** | 0 | 0 | 1 | 0 | 0 | 0 | 0 | 0 | 0 | – | 1 |

a–Flew out for Meacham in 9th.

Chicago	IP	H	R	ER	BB	SO
Seaver (W)	9	6	1	1	1	7

New York						
Cowley (L)	5 1/3	7	2	2	5	2
Fisher	2/3	4	2	2	1	0
Shirley	2	2	0	0	0	2
Allen	1	0	0	0	0	1

DP–Yankees 1. LOB–Chicago 10, New York 8. E–Hulett. 2B–Salazar, Hulett, Fisk.
HBP–Randloph (by Seaver). T–3:20. A–54,032.

Phil Niekro

King of the Knuckleballers

Of all the pitches that have been projected toward home plate during the course of baseball's lengthy history, none was ever more difficult to throw—or to hit or to catch—than the knuckleball. It is a pitch that defies all the qualities of convenience.

For that reason, few pitchers have used it. Even fewer have mastered it. The knuckleball is really a freak pitch that thrives on abnormal behavior. It is unpredictable, and often unmanageable. And seldom does one knuckleball resemble the previous one.

Because the pitch flutters plateward usually at 50 to 55 miles per hour and lacks the macho stature of a 95 mph fastball, knuckleball users are kind of like the Rodney Dangerfields of the pitching fraternity. They get no respect. They're treated more like the sideshow performers at a circus. Never has anyone ever ranked a knuckleball hurler among baseball's greatest pitchers.

Incredibly, **Phil Niekro** won his 300th game without using his knuckleball until the end.

An exception, however, could be made for Phil Niekro. He is the only knuckleball hurler ever to win 300 games, compiling a 318–274 record. He pitched in the major leagues for 24 years. He was a 20-game winner three times and reached double figures in wins 19 times. And he is a member of the Hall of Fame, having been inducted in 1997 after getting 380 votes on 473 ballots cast.

The knuckleball, a pitch that dates back to the early 1900s, wasn't Niekro's only pitch. But he threw it 75 to 80 percent of the time. Unlike other devotees of the flutterball, Phil threw his with a stiff wrist, holding the ball with his fingertips. With no spin, the pitch would wobble toward the plate, dancing and juking as it came, and then when it neared the batter, it would suddenly and without warning dart one way or another, leaving a frustrated hitter and often a catcher trying to figure out where the ball went.

"Trying to hit him is like trying to eat Jello with chopsticks," outfielder Bobby Murcer once said. So mysterious was the pitch that one of Niekro's catchers, Bob Uecker, once chased the ball back to the screen behind home plate only to find it was in his glove all the time. "I have no idea which way the thing is going to go," Uecker said.

While the knuckleball pandered to longevity—two of the other great knuckleball hurlers, Hoyt Wilhelm and Emil (Dutch) Leonard, pitched for 21 and 20 years, respectively—the uncertainty of its flight always created control problems for the user. In Niekro's case, he issued the third highest total of walks (1,809), and ranks sixth in wild pitches (226) in big league history. Once, he tossed six wild pitches in a game, including four in one inning.

The 6-foot, 1-inch, 180-pound Niekro is among the all-time leaders in numerous other categories, too. He is tied for second in most 200-inning seasons (19), ranks third in most games (864) for a nonreliever, most hits allowed (5,044), and most home runs yielded (482), is fourth in games started (716) and innings pitched (5,404.1), is fifth in losses, and is eighth in strikeouts (3,342).

Niekro toiled primarily for the Atlanta Braves, a franchise for which he is regarded as one of its most popular and outstanding players. He performed his accomplishments after not reaching the majors to stay until he was 28 years old and while laboring for mostly mediocre to bad teams. His career winning percentage of .537 is significantly higher than that of the teams for which he pitched. Phil won more games (114) after the age of 40 than any other pitcher. He also authored a no-hitter, was chosen for five All-Star games, appearing in two of them, and won five Gold Gloves. And with his brother Joe, winner of 221 games, the Niekros are the winningest brother combination in major league history, with 539 triumphs.

The winningest brother combination, Joe (left) and **Phil Niekro** get together with parents.

Perhaps the oddest event in Niekro's career came when he delivered his 300th win. It came on October 6, 1985, when, while wearing the uniform of the New York Yankees, he defeated the newly crowned American League East Division champion Toronto Blue Jays, 8–0, at Exhibition Stadium. Toronto had just clinched the title one day earlier, and many of its regulars were not in the lineup.

The win made Phil, at the age of 46, the oldest pitcher ever to toss a shutout. Aside from the fact that it came after four futile tries at winning his 300th, what made the game especially remarkable was that in allowing just four hits, striking out five, and walking three, Niekro went practically the whole distance without using his venerable knuckleball. He threw sinking fastballs, curves, screwballs, and even some blooper pitches, but shunned use of his trademark knuckler until he struck out Jeff Burroughs with three of them with two outs in the ninth inning.

"I always wanted to pitch a whole game without throwing knuckleballs because people thought I couldn't get batters out without throwing them," *New York Times* reporter Murray Chass quoted Niekro as telling perplexed writers afterward. "So today, I said, 'let's go out in the first inning and see if I can get them out without throwing a knuckleball.' I did, so I didn't throw any in the second inning and then I went from there. In the ninth, I decided if I was going to win the 300th, I should finish with a knuckleball. I figured there was no other way to finish the game than using the pitch that got me there."

Harry Cotto's two-run single in the first, Mike Pagliarulo's two-run, pinch-hit homer in the fifth, a two-run homer in the eighth by Cotto—his first in the big leagues—and Don Mattingly's solo blast in the ninth led the offense for the Yankees, who finished two games behind Toronto. In the ninth, Niekro's brother and teammate, Joe, warmed up Phil before the inning.

What the game showed, said Niekro, "is that you don't have to throw the ball 95 miles an hour and have a Dwight Gooden curveball to pitch in the majors." For Niekro, who never missed a turn because of arm trouble, the statement was indisputable.

But it had not been easy reaching that point. Born April 1, 1939, Phil grew up the son of a poor coal miner in the eastern Ohio town of Bridgeport. One of Phil's high school teammates was a kid named John Havlicek, a guy who would be heard from again as one of the all-time greats of the Boston Celtics.

The Niekros had no car and no telephone. "There really wasn't much going on, so we had nothing else to do but play baseball, think baseball, and practice baseball," Phil said.

Fortunately, Phil's father, also Phil, had been a pretty good sandlot pitcher, and he taught his sons the knuckleball. Phil began throwing the pitch when he was eight.

"I'd be carrying a lunch pail today without it," Phil said. "I couldn't throw hard enough—I had just an average fastball and curve—so I learned to throw the knuckleball most of the time. But it always mystified me. One time it'll zoom down. Next time, it zooms up."

Turning down a college basketball scholarship after averaging 20 points per game in high school, Niekro was signed by the Milwaukee Braves at a tryout camp in Ohio. He was sent to Wellsville in the New York Penn League, but eventually was released. Phil pleaded with the Braves for another chance. Taken back and placed at McCook in the Nebraska State League, he then embarked on an odyssey that over a five-year period took him all over the country. Used mostly as a reliever, he never won more than nine games (at Louisville in 1962) before entering military service in 1963.

Phil showed up briefly in Milwaukee in 1964 but spent most of the season with Denver of the Pacific Coast League, going 11–5. He lasted the whole season in 1965 with the Braves, getting his first major league win. But after the Braves moved to Atlanta in 1966, Niekro wound up at Richmond at mid-season.

By 1967, Niekro had pitched in 79 games for the Braves but started exactly once. The '67 season, however, proved to be the turning point in his career. Starting 20 of the 46 games he worked, Niekro led the National League with a glittering 1.87 earned run average while posting an 11–9 record that included an 8–3 victory over the Chicago Cubs and brother Joe, who was starting his first big league game. Phil would seldom relieve again.

He went to 14–12 in 1968, then had one of the finest seasons of his career when he checked in with a 23–13 mark that included 21 complete games. That season, the heretofore lowly Braves reached the first National League playoffs but were swept in three games by the Miracle Mets of New York, with Niekro absorbing a 9–5 loss in the opener after getting touched for five unearned runs in the eighth inning.

An appendectomy helped to drop Niekro's record to 12–18 in 1970. Over the next three years, he would win 44 games, including a 2–1 victory over the Philadelphia Phillies in 1972 that broke Steve Carlton's 15-game winning streak.

In 1973, Niekro, the owner of an outstanding pickoff move to first, became the first Atlanta Braves pitcher to fire a no-hitter when he beat the San Diego Padres, 9–0. Phil struck out four and walked three while becoming one of the few knuckleball hurlers ever to no-hit the opposition.

Niekro had another big year in 1974 when he went 20–13 and led the league in complete games (18) and innings pitched (302). It would be the first of four times that Phil worked in more than 300 innings, leading the league each time. Overall, "Knucksie," as he was sometimes called, would also lead the league in games started and complete games, each four times, and in hits allowed and walks, three times apiece.

Phil lost 20 games in 1977 (winning 16) while leading the league in strikeouts (262) for the only time in his career, then posted a 19–18 mark the following year. In 1979, in one of his more unusual seasons, Niekro came up with a 21–20 record for the last-place Braves, leading the league in wins, losses, games started (44), complete games (23), innings pitched (342), hits (311), and walks (113).

Over a four-year period between 1977 and 1980, Niekro would win 71 games for the hapless Braves. But he'd also lose 76, leading the league in that category each time.

His last big year for Atlanta came in 1982, when he had a 17–4 record with a league-leading .810 winning percentage. That year, Phil not only captured his 250th career win, he returned to the National League playoffs. Again, however, the Braves were swept in three games, this time by the St. Louis Cardinals. Niekro, whose 1–0 lead in the first game was washed out by rain in the fifth inning, got no decision in Game Two, departing after six innings with a 3–2 lead that Gene Garber turned into a 4–3 Braves loss.

After one more season in Atlanta, the Braves decided that Niekro had outlived his usefulness and released him. Although 45, Phil was far from through. Signed by the Yankees, he fashioned a combined 32–20 record over the next two years. In one game in 1984, a 5–0 decision over the Texas Rangers, he became the ninth pitcher in major league history to record 3,000 strikeouts.

Even after winning his 300th game and getting waived by the Yankees in spring training the following year, Niekro still had some life left in his well-used arm. Six days later, he joined the Cleveland Indians and went 11–11 for the year. In one game, Niekro faced Don Sutton of the California Angels (neither was involved in the decision) in the first confrontation of 300-game winners since Tim Keefe and Pud Galvin squared off in 1892.

Phil began the 1987 season with the Indians, along the way winning his 318th and final game. But before the campaign was over, he had been released, picked up for a brief fling with the Blue Jays, then tossed a ceremonial final game back with the Braves, after which he retired.

A man noted for his high character both on and off the field, Niekro participated in many charitable and community activities during and after his career. He won numerous honors for his work, including the Brian Piccolo Award, the Lou Gehrig Memorial Award, and the Roberto Clemente Award.

Niekro tried his hand at managing in the 1990s, piloting the Braves Triple-A club at Richmond in 1990 and the Silver Bullets, a women's professional team, in 1994. In recent years, the Braves have honored their top minor league pitcher with a trophy called the Phil Niekro Award. The award couldn't have a more appropriate namesake.

October 6, 1985—Yankees 8, Blue Jays 0

New York	AB	R	H	RBI	Toronto	AB	R	H	RBI
Henderson, cf	3	0	0	0	Garcia, 2b	3	0	0	0
Pasqua, lf	2	0	0	0	G. Iorg, 2b	1	0	0	0
Mattingly, 1b	5	3	4	1	Leach, lf	3	0	0	0
Winfield, rf	5	0	0	0	L. Thornton, rf	4	0	0	0
Baylor, dh	4	1	0	0	Fielder, 1b	2	0	1	0
Robertson, 3b	2	1	0	0	b–Fernandez, ph	1	0	1	0
a–Pagliarulo, 3b	3	1	1	2	Burroughs, dh	4	0	1	0
Randolph, 2b	0	1	0	1	Gruber, 3b	3	0	0	0
Cotto, lf	4	1	2	4	Shepherd, cf	3	0	0	0
Wynegar, c	3	0	0	0	Hearron, c	3	0	0	0
Meacham, ss	4	0	0	0	Lee, ss	2	0	1	0
Totals	35	8	7	8		29	0	4	0

New York	3	0	0	0	2	0	0	2	1	–	8	
Toronto	0	0	0	0	0	0	0	0	0	–	0	

a–Homered for Robertson in 5th.
b–Doubled for Fielder in 9th.

New York	IP	H	R	ER	BB	SO
Niekro (W)	9	4	0	0	3	5
Toronto						
Cerutti (L)	4	2	3	0	3	3
Acker	2	2	2	2	1	2
Caudill	2	2	2	2	1	0
S. Davis	1	1	1	1	0	1

DP–New York 2. LOB–New York 6, Toronto 5. E–Garcia. 2B–Burroughs, Fernandez. HR - Pagliarulo, Cotto, Mattingly. SB–Randolph. HBP–Randolph (by Cerutti). Wild Pitches–Cerutti 2. T–2:25. A–44,472.

Don Sutton

Never Missed a Turn

Many words have been used to describe big league pitchers. Some fit; some don't. But there is no need to struggle for an appropriate portrayal of Don Sutton. He was consistent and he was dependable.

Calling a pitcher consistent and dependable may be the ultimate compliment. All kinds of flattery can be tossed a hurler's way, but nothing is more satisfactory nor lifts his spirits higher than a favorable acclamation of his work ethic.

And Sutton certainly had an exemplary work ethic. The 6-foot, 1-inch, 185-pounder never missed a turn in the starting rotation in 23 years. When he was supposed to pitch, he pitched. Nothing, neither illness nor injury, neither bad weather, jet lag, nor anything else ever kept Don from keeping an appointment on the mound.

Sutton, who spent the first 15 years of his career with the Los Angeles Dodgers before playing with four other teams, never spent a day on the disabled list until the last two months of his career. He

Don Sutton never missed a starting assignment in 23 seasons in the majors.

made more than 30 starts in 20 different seasons. He worked in more than 200 innings 20 different years, an achievement topped by no other major league pitcher.

But Sutton was not just reliable. He made it a practice of winning the big games. "I think he's the best money pitcher in baseball," Dodgers manager Tom Lasorda once said.

Sutton thrived on pressure. He was known as an extremely tough competitor who throughout his career was usually assigned to pitch his team's biggest games. When it came to doing his job, no pitcher was ever more focused than the slender righthander.

"The tougher the game, the better he got," said Walter Alston, Sutton's first Dodgers manager. "When the game is on the line,"

Alston wrote in a book he gave to Don, "I want you to have the ball."

Sutton had the ball so often that he finished his lengthy career with a 324–256 record. He ranks third on the all-time list in games started with 756, fifth in strikeouts with 3,574, seventh in innings pitched with 5,282.1, and 10th in shutouts with 58. Sutton struck out more than 100 batters in each of his first 21 seasons. And he beat every major league team of his era at least once.

Overall, Sutton appeared in 774 games, completing 178 of his starts. His career earned run average was 3.26, which included eight times under 3.00, and he allowed 4,692 hits while walking 1,343. He hurled five one-hitters and nine two-hitters. Don was elected to the Hall of Fame in 1998 after receiving 386 votes with 473 ballots cast.

Although many superb pitchers have worn the Dodgers uniform over the years—Dazzy Vance, Burleigh Grimes, Sandy Koufax, Don Drysdale, and Orel Hershiser to name a few—Sutton leads the franchise in virtually every major mound category. Ironically, although Don reached double figures in wins 21 times, he was a 20-game winner only once. No other 300-game winner had as few 20-win seasons.

"I just want to be remembered as one of the most dependable pitchers this club has produced. I'm part of a team. I work hard. I contribute what I can, and what happens, happens," Sutton said in defense of his paucity of 20-win seasons. "You can go nothing-nothing for 27 innings and not win. Sometimes, winning is out of a pitcher's hands."

Sutton's hands possessed a variety of offerings. He threw five different pitches, including a good but not overpowering fastball, a slider, screwball, and changeup. His best pitch was a curve. "I don't think too many pitchers have mastered as many pitches as he has," Alston said.

With excellent control, Sutton liked to nibble at the corners of the plate, moving the ball in and out and up and down, trying to make the batters hit his pitch. "It took me some time to realize that it is easier and less exhausting to get a man out on a grounder than to try to blow a fastball by him," Don said.

Sutton was occasionally accused of scuffing the ball, and he was ejected from a game in 1978 when it was alleged that he applied more than his fingertips to the surface. Don, however, was issued nothing more severe than a warning after he threatened to file a lawsuit against the umpire who threw him out. Later, Sutton joked about doctoring balls, saying that he once received a jar of Vaseline from Gaylord Perry in exchange for a piece of sandpaper.

Jokes were always a part of Sutton's persona. Urbane and articulate, Don was an avid practical joker who once removed the wheels from Alston's golf cart and another time glued the bullpen telephone to the receiver. Sutton was also a guy who took a cold shower before pitching each game and chewed black olives rather than gum or tobacco. He was a devoted physical fitness buff, too.

Sutton's biggest game unquestionably came on June 18, 1986, when as a California Angel he was credited with his 300th victory, firing a three-hitter to beat the Texas Rangers, 5–1, at Anaheim Stadium. Ever the master of efficiency, the 41-year-old hurler needed just 85 pitches to win his second straight complete game. Nine days earlier, Sutton had captured his 299th decision with a two-hit, 3–0, complete game victory over the Chicago White Sox.

Rob Wilfong's two-run single helped the Angels take a 3–0 lead in the first inning. Solo home runs by Ruppert Jones in the fifth and Brian Downing in the seventh completed the Angels' scoring. At one point, Sutton retired 15 Rangers in a row. He finished with three strikeouts while walking none.

Don was born April 2, 1945, in Clio, Alabama, but spent most of his formative years growing up on a farm in Molina, Florida. After graduating from high school in Pensacola, Florida, he attended Gulf Coast Community College, Mississippi College, the University of Southern California, and Whittier College. Scouts who watched him pitch were not enthusiastic about his chances because they said he was too small and didn't throw hard enough.

With a game on the line, Walter Alston said he wanted **Don Sutton** to have the ball.

The Dodgers finally took a chance on Sutton, signing him as a free agent in 1964. In his first year in pro ball in 1965, Don divided his time between Santa Barbara of the California League and Albuquerque of the Texas League, putting together a combined 23–7 record while being named Texas League Player of the Year for his 15–6 mark there.

With just one year of minor league experience, the 21-year-old hurler made the big club in 1966. He was an instant success. Sutton won his first game, a 6–3 decision over the Houston Astros. With some special tutoring from Koufax, he went on to post a 12–12 record while striking out 209 batters. That was not only the highest total for a rookie since Grover Cleveland Alexander fanned 227 in 1911; it helped to earn Sutton *The Sporting News* National League Rookie of the Year Award.

The Dodgers won the National League pennant that year but were swept by the Baltimore Orioles in the World Series. Don saw no action. At that point, he was the fourth member of a marvelous pitching staff that included Koufax, Drysdale, and Claude Osteen. When Koufax retired after the season, Sutton moved up a notch in the rotation, but over the next three years he had losing seasons, recording identical 11–15 marks and a 17–18 log in 1969.

Despite his records, Sutton was making a favorable impression on National League hitters. "He knows what he's doing," said home run king Hank Aaron. "He doesn't back down. He's confident, poised, and throws strikes."

Throwing strikes is something Don's sixth grade coach had urged him to do, and finally in 1970, the advice started to pay off. Sutton began a streak of winning seasons that would take him through most of the decade.

In 1972, he had his first big season, going 19–9 with a 2.08 ERA and leading the league with nine shutouts. That year, he was named to his first of four All-Star teams. Then, after registering an 18–10 mark the following season, he was back at 19–9 in 1974. Sutton led the league in starts with 40, one of only three times in his entire career that he led his peers in any category.

The 1974 season turned out to be an especially noteworthy one for Sutton. His four-hit shutout beat the Pittsburgh Pirates, 3–0, in the opener of the National League Championship Series. Four days later, he worked eight innings to get the win in the fourth and deciding game as the Dodgers rode Steve Garvey's two homers and four RBI to a 12–1 triumph. In the World Series against the Oakland Athletics, the Dodgers won only once, and that was a 3–2 decision that went to Sutton in the second game.

Sutton's only 20-win season came in 1976, when he posted a 21–10 record for the NL West's second-place Dodgers in Alston's last season as manager. Don gained his 20th win with a six-hit, 3–1 victory over the San Francisco Giants. He would then go on to register 166 wins during the decade.

There were many milestones along the way. In 1977, Sutton was the starting and winning pitcher in the National League's 7–5 triumph in the All-Star Game, hurling three scoreless innings as his team jumped out to a 4–0 lead in the first. Don was named the game's Most Valuable Player. The game marked Sutton's fourth appearance as an All-Star and ran his scoreless streak in the midsummer classic to eight innings.

That year, Sutton also went the distance to beat the Philadelphia Phillies, 7–1, in the second game of the NLCS. After winning the playoffs in four games, the Dodgers bowed to the New York Yankees in six games in the World Series. Sutton started the first game but was not involved in the decision in the Dodgers' 4–3 loss. He then gained the decision in Game Five with a complete game, 10–4 victory.

Sutton suffered the only LCS loss of his career and the Dodgers' only loss of the series in 1978 when he bowed to Steve Carlton and the Phillies, 9–4, in the third game. In the World Series, Don was on the losing end of a 5–1 count in the third game and a 7–2 score in the sixth and deciding game against the winning Yankees.

Three years later, having led the league in ERA with a 2.20 in 1980, Sutton's Dodgers career came to a stunning end. Don became a free agent after the 1981 season, and after futilely negotiating with the Atlanta Braves, he wound up signing a four-year contract with Houston. He won 24 games for the Astros in a little less than two years before getting traded late in the 1982 season to the Milwaukee Brewers, a team fighting for the American League East Division pennant.

In one of the most satisfying games of his career, Sutton—with Robin Yount slugging two home runs and a triple—defeated Jim

Palmer and the Baltimore Orioles, 10–2, to clinch the flag for the Brewers. It was Don's fourth win in five decisions since joining Milwaukee.

With the Brewers down two games to none to the Angels in the American League Championship Series, Sutton staved off his team's elimination with a 5–3 victory. The Brewers then won two more games to reach the World Series against the St. Louis Cardinals. Sutton started but got no decision in a 5–4 loss in Game Two, then was routed, 13–1, in the sixth game as the Cardinals came back to take the Series in seven games.

He posted a 17–9 record for the Astros and Brewers in 1982, but Sutton's streak of 17 straight seasons with wins in double figures ended the following year, when he slipped to 8–13. Don bounced back to 14–12 in 1984. He then won in double figures three more times while pitching for the Athletics and Angels.

Sutton, who won 44 games after the age of 40, wound up back with the Dodgers in 1988 in what was his final year in the big leagues. Now 43, he retired at the end of the season.

Having long been interested in a television career following his retirement as a player, Sutton got his wish in 1989 when he was hired as a color man by the Braves. He has held that post since then while also expanding his duties to include the broadcasting of professional golf tournaments.

June 18, 1986—Angels 5, Rangers 1

Texas	AB	R	H	RBI	California	AB	H	R	RBI
McDowell cf	4	0	0	0	Pettis, cf	3	1	1	0
Ward, lf	4	0	0	0	Joyner, 1b	4	0	1	0
O'Brien, 1b	3	0	0	0	Downing, lf	4	2	2	2
Incaviglia, dh	3	1	1	1	R. Jackson, dh	4	1	1	0
Parrish, 3b	3	0	0	0	R. Jones, rf	2	1	1	1
Sierra, rf	3	0	2	0	DeCinces, 3b	3	0	1	0
Harrah, 2b	3	0	0	0	Wilfong, 2b	4	0	2	2
Petralli, c	3	0	0	0	Schofield, ss	3	0	0	0
Fletcher, ss	3	0	0	0	Boone, c	4	0	0	0
Totals	29	1	3	1		31	5	9	5

Texas	0 0 0 0 0 0 1 0 0	–	1
California	3 0 0 0 1 0 1 0 x	–	5

Texas	IP	H	R	ER	BB	SO
Guzman (L)	6 2/3	8	5	5	3	3
M. Williams	1 1/3	1	0	0	2	0

California						
Sutton (W)	9	3	1	1	0	3

DP–Texas 2, California 1. LOB–Texas 1, California 7. E–Fletcher. 2B–Wilfong. HR–R. Jones, Incaviglia, Downing. SB–Downing, Pettis. T–2:13. A–37,044.

Nolan Ryan

Strikeout Specialist

Whenever the great strikeout pitchers in baseball are discussed, one name dominates the conversation. The name Nolan Ryan is synonymous with the special knack of firing a third strike past a batter.

Ryan was certifiably the King of Ks. While he was by no means the only towering figure in the strikeout market, he was by far the best. Strikeouts and Ryan were linked together as integrally as nails are to a carpenter.

The record speaks clearly. Ryan's 5,714 career strikeouts are the highest total in major league history. His single-season mark of 383 whiffs is the highest since the 19th century. He holds major league records for most seasons with 100 or more (24), 200 or more (15), and 300 or more (six) strikeouts. Twenty-six times, he fanned 15 or more in one game, and 215 times he struck out 10 or more in one game—both all-time records.

Nolan Ryan struck out more batters than any pitcher in history.

Ryan whiffed 19 batters in a single game four times. He fanned 18 batters in a game once, 17 on three occasions, and 16 eight times. During his entire career, he averaged 9.55 kayos a game. Nolan led his league in strikeouts 11 times. On 331 different occasions, he struck out the side. Ryan counted among his strikeout victims 12 sets of brothers and eight father and son combinations.

The strikeout records of the 6-foot, 2-inch, 210-pound righthander are of such monumental proportions that no other pitcher's strikeouts are even remotely close. Ryan, for instance, has nearly 1,600 more strikeouts than the second-highest total. And no one ever fanned batters past the age of 40 the way Nolan did.

It helped, of course, that Ryan had one of the fiercest fastballs ever launched. He also owned a dazzling curve and later in his career a devilish changeup. But the fastball was Nolan's best friend. At its peak, it rocketed toward the plate at laser-like speeds, often exceeding 100 miles per hour. Ryan put so much effort into throwing his fastball that he grunted loudly when he unleashed it. Hitters cringed. Bats shattered. Catchers' mitts ripped apart.

"This is a man who throws the fastest ball I've ever seen," said Hall of Famer Red Schoendienst, who spent more than 50 years in the big leagues as a player, coach, manager, and executive. "He's just overpowering," added Hall of Fame slugger Harmon Killebrew. "It's almost sinful for a pitcher to have his combination of speed and stuff."

Batting against Ryan and catching him weren't the only formidable tasks. Umpires struggled to see his pitches and make the calls. "Either his fastball or his curve should be outlawed. They're that tough," umpire Ron Luciano once said.

"A lot of people think I really tried to strike out people, but that's not the case," Ryan told Ron Smith of *The Sporting News*. "I was just a strikeout-style pitcher. My really high totals come when hitters are looking for my fastball and I'm getting my breaking ball over the plate."

Ryan attributed much of his success to his conditioning. He was fanatical about staying in shape all year long and worked feverishly to accomplish that goal. "It all starts with the legs," he said. "They're the foundation." Although he made 16 trips to the disabled list during his career, Nolan seldom sat down because of an arm problem.

The marvelous condition of his body, coupled with his intense mental approach, not only made Ryan the perfect definition of a

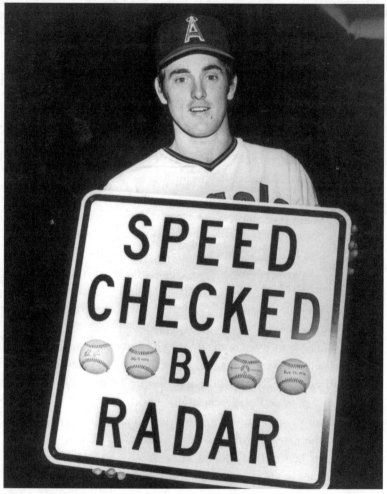

Speed was a quality that **Nolan Ryan** had in abundance.

power pitcher, they gave his career longevity. Even with the heavy toll that his deliveries took on his arm, the flame-throwing hurler appeared in the major leagues in 27 seasons—more than any other player in history.

While accumulating a 324–292 won-lost total with the New York Mets, California Angels, Houston Astros, and Texas Rangers, Ryan set more than 50 all-time records. In addition to his strikeout marks, he holds the record for most no-hitters, with seven, and most low-hit games, with 19. Ryan fired 12 one-hitters (he also recorded 19 two-hitters and 30 three-hitters). Among other significant marks, he ranks first in the major leagues in consecutive starting assignments (595), walks (2,795), and wild pitches (277). He is second on the all-time list in games started (773), third in losses, fifth in innings pitched (5,386), and tied for seventh in shutouts (61).

Overall, Ryan appeared in 807 games, starting 773 and completing 222. He gave up 3,923 hits while registering a career earned run average of 3.19. Opposing hitters batted just .204 against Nolan during his career. He worked in more than 300 innings in one season twice and more than 200 innings 14 times. Nolan won in double figures 20 times. He was a member of eight All-Star teams, appearing in five of them, including a starting assignment in 1979.

One of Ryan's most remarkable achievements was his seven no-hitters (he lost five other no-hit bids in the ninth inning), the first four of which came while he was with the Angels. In 1973, he became only the fifth pitcher in baseball history to toss two no-hitters in the same season when he beat the Kansas City Royals, 3–0, on May 15 and the Detroit Tigers, 6–0, on July 15, fanning 17, including eight straight in that game. Nolan beat the Minnesota Twins, 4–0, on September 28, 1974, for his third no-hitter, then blanked the Baltimore Orioles, 1–0, on June 1, 1975, for his fourth whitewash.

After he moved to Houston, his fifth no-hitter came on September 26, 1981, with a 5–0 victory over the Los Angeles Dodgers. Ryan's last two no-hitters came with the Rangers. On July 11, 1990, he blitzed the Oakland Athletics, 5–0, to become at the age of 43 the oldest pitcher ever to hurl a no-hitter and the first to hurl such a game in three different decades. The following season, on May 1, 1991, he zapped the Toronto Blue Jays, 3–0, with a 16-strikeout masterpiece that Ryan said was his strongest no-hit performance.

Ryan was elected to the Hall of Fame in 1999, collecting 491 votes out of a possible 497. Only Tom Seaver had a higher percentage of votes cast than Ryan's 98.79.

It was a spot in which he never expected to find himself. "When I was an active player, I concerned myself with the job I had to do," he told the Dallas *Morning News*. "I was never one who reminisced on what happened in my career. I was just concerned with today and what I had to do for tomorrow."

As a youngster, he was an easy-going country boy from Alvin, Texas, near where he was born January 31, 1947. Even as a kid, though, Ryan could throw incredibly hard. He threw so hard that once, in a high school game, he broke a batter's arm with a pitch, then cracked the next batter's helmet.

Veteran Mets scout Red Murff spotted Ryan in a high school game and was so impressed by the boy's fastball that he sent back a report that said: "This skinny kid has the best arm I have ever seen in my life." Murff stayed on Ryan's trail, and in 1965, the Mets drafted the 18-year-old Texan in the eighth round. Nolan got a $12,000 bonus and $500 per month.

Ryan was just a thrower, and it showed as he was plagued by wildness. But he struck out 115 in 78 innings in his first year at Marion in the Appalachian League and 272 in 183 innings while compiling a 17–2 record the next year at Greenville in the Western Carolina League. After a brief stint at Williamsport, he came up to the Mets in 1966 but appeared in only two games before dividing the following season between Winter Haven, Jacksonville, the disabled list, and a stint in the military.

The young fireballer, who soaked the fingers of his pitching hand in pickle juice to fend off a chronic blister problem, made the big leagues to stay in 1968. Because he was still attached to a reserve unit that required him to serve in Houston every other weekend, Ryan got only 18 starts and posted a 6–9 record. The following year he split his time between starting and relieving but managed only a 6–3 mark. That fall, however, Nolan pitched seven innings of three-hit relief to get the win in the Mets 7–4 victory over the Atlanta Braves in the third and deciding game of the first National League Championship Series. Then, in the only World Series appearance of his career, he earned a save in a 5–0 triumph in the third game of the Miracle Mets five-game victory over the Baltimore Orioles.

Ryan, though, was growing increasingly unhappy. After winning 17 and losing 25 over the next two years, he asked to be traded. "I was frustrated with the fact that I was not progressing as a pitcher," he said. He also disliked New York City.

Following the 1971 season, the Mets traded Ryan and three other players to the Angels for over-the-hill infielder Jim Fregosi in what was the worst swap in the franchise's history. With the Angels, Ryan came under the tutelage of pitching coach Tom Morgan, who Nolan would later say "took me on as a project and turned my career around."

Morgan showed Ryan how to be a pitcher. The results took immediate effect. "I really got to where I understood my delivery and started to get consistent with my stuff," Nolan said. He posted a 19–16 record in 1972, then had the only 20-win seasons of his career when he went 21–16 and 22–16 in the next two years. Over the ensuing five years, covering the most successful period in his career, Ryan won 76 games while losing 73.

No-hitters, big strikeout games, and a 100.8 mph clocking of his fastball—the fastest pitch ever recorded—highlighted Ryan's portfolio with the Angels. In one game in 1974, he fanned 19 batters for the first time in a 4–2 shredding of the Boston Red Sox. Nolan's three other 19-K games were extra-inning affairs.

So intimidating was the Ryan Express, as Nolan's work came to be named, that Hall of Famer Reggie Jackson said: "Ryan's the only guy who puts fear in me. Not because he could get me out, but because he could kill me. You just hoped to mix in a walk so you could have a good night and go 0 for 3."

Although he made hitters tremble, Ryan had his share of critics who during most of his career complained that Nolan was merely a .500 pitcher despite his no-hitters and strikeouts. Ryan answered by pointing out that, through most of his career, he was pitching "for bad teams." The truth was, Ryan had a higher winning percentage than the combined winning percentage of all the teams on which he played.

"My attitude about pitching," he told Michael Schwager in *Phillies Report*, "is I give the team I'm pitching for the opportunity to win the ball game. I don't have much to do with the offense. I'm a defensive specialist. That's my job. If I do fine, we have a chance to win. If we lose, either we didn't score runs or I didn't do my job. I don't worry about the win-loss record."

In 1980, Ryan got to play on one of his few successful teams when he became a free agent and signed baseball's first $1 million contract with the Astros. He played nine years in Houston, winning 106 games and losing 94, his best season being a 16–12 mark in 1982. In 1983, he broke Walter Johnson's all-time strikeout record, and two years later he became the first hurler ever to register 4,000 kayos.

Incredibly, Ryan was paid the same salary every year. But in 1988 when Houston tried to assess a 20 percent pay cut, Nolan rejoined the free-agent market and signed with the Rangers. In his first season with Texas, Ryan posted a 16–10 record and at the age of 42 became the oldest pitcher ever to win an All-Star Game as the American League captured a 5–3 victory at Anaheim. He also became the oldest hurler ever to strike out more than 300 batters when he fanned 301 while also notching his 5,000th whiff.

"It helps if the hitter thinks you're a little crazy," Ryan once said. He was referring to his work on the mound. But some people also thought he was a little crazy to keep pitching well into his mid-40s. Nolan merely shrugged and continued to defy the odds.

His crowning achievement came on July 31, 1990, when he won his 300th game with an 11–3 decision over the Milwaukee Brewers at County Stadium. The win came on his second attempt and made Ryan the 20th and last hurler to achieve 300 victories.

Ryan, who was cheered throughout the game, worked seven and two-thirds innings, throwing 146 pitches, allowing six hits, striking out eight, and walking two before being lifted with two men on base and after giving up two unearned runs in the eighth. The Rangers made Ryan's job easy, with Jeff Huson's two-run triple sparking a four-run fifth and a six-run ninth that featured Julio Franco's grand-slam home run.

"I'm relieved that it's over," Nolan said afterward. "The last 15 days probably have been as tough emotionally as any 15 days I've gone through. It was a physically demanding game. What was really exciting was the Milwaukee fans being so supportive. It speaks well of them as a baseball community."

Ryan's fastball was still being clocked in the upper 90s range when he won that game. He continued to throw with blinding speed until injuries began slowing him down in 1992. Nolan made his final appearance on September 22, 1993, when he tore a ligament in his elbow in the first inning. Shortly thereafter, he retired, having won only five games in each of his last two seasons. In five years with the Rangers, he was 51–39—not bad for a guy who was 46 when he fired his last pitch.

July 31, 1990—Rangers 11, Brewers 3

Texas	AB	R	H	RBI	Milwaukee	AB	R	H	RBI
Huson, ss	4	0	1	2	Molitor, 1b	5	2	3	0
a–Daugherty, ph	1	1	1	1	Yount, cf	5	1	1	1
Green, ss	0	0	0	0	Sheffield, 3b	4	0	0	0
Franco, 2b	5	1	1	4	Parker, dh	4	0	1	0
Palmeiro, 1b	5	0	2	0	Vaughn, lf	4	0	0	0
Sierra, rf	5	2	3	0	Gantner, 2b	3	0	2	1
Baines, dh	5	1	1	0	Felder, rf	3	0	0	0
Incaviglia, lf	3	2	2	2	O'Brien, c	3	0	0	0
Petralli, c	2	1	0	1	b–Hamilton, ph	1	0	0	0
Buechele, 3b	4	2	2	1	Spiers, ss	4	0	0	0
Pettis, cf	3	1	0	0					
Totals	37	11	13	11		36	3	7	2

Texas	0	0	0	0	4	1	0	0	6	–	11	
Milwaukee	0	0	1	0	0	0	0	2	0	–	3	

a–Singled for Huson in 9th.
b–Batted for O'Brien in 9th.

Texas	IP	H	R	ER	BB	SO
Ryan (W)	7 2/3	6	3	1	2	8
Arnsberg (S)	1 1/3	1	0	0	0	0

Milwaukee						
Bosio (L)	5 1/3	6	5	5	1	1
Mirabella	2 2/3	4	2	2	1	1
Knudson	0	1	2	1	0	0
Fossas	1	2	2	2	0	1

Mirabella pitched to two batters in 9th. Knudson pitched to two batters in 9th.

DP–Milwaukee 1. LOB–Texas 3, Milwaukee 8. E–Buechele, Franco 2, Knudson. 2B–Sierra. 3B–Yount, Huson, Palmeiro. HR–Incaviglia, Franco. SB–Gantner. S–Pettis. SF–Petralli. Wild Pitch–Ryan. T–3:05. A–51,533.

Are 300-Game Winners a Vanishing Breed?

After the next few years, will anyone ever win 300 games again? Or is the 300-game winner a vanishing breed that will soon make its final appearance?

There is, of course, no conclusive answer. But the question is one that a book of this kind needs to address. It is an especially significant question as the sport of baseball continues to undergo dramatic changes as it moves deeper into the twenty-first century.

No part of the sport has been subjected to more substantial alterations than what takes place on the pitching mound. Sure, a strike is still a strike, and it takes three of them to record an out. But the whole system of pitching has changed considerably in recent years, and those changes could have a strong bearing on the existence of future 300-game winners.

Without getting too technical, it could be said that, despite the differences in eras, there was little variation between the way Cy Young and the way Tom Seaver went about their jobs. Likewise, whether it was Eddie Plank, Lefty Grove, or Warren Spahn, they all worked in similar ways.

Such comparisons, however, do not in most cases include current pitchers. They operate on a different level than their predecessors.

It is not the process of delivering a baseball to home plate that has changed so much. It is the combination of factors surrounding the business of pitching that is different. And that includes not only the physical aspects of the job, but also the mental approach.

The two-man pitching staff of Old Hoss Radbourn's day yielded to the four-man starting rotation through much of the 20th century, and that in turn has now been replaced by five-man staffs of starters. Instead of pitching every other day or even every fourth day, pitchers now work every five or six days. Automatically, that reduces the number of starts—and decisions—for today's pitchers.

In general, starting pitchers today are also getting fewer wins because they complete fewer games. While once Walter Johnson annually completed upwards of 30 games—and a complete game was treated as a badge of honor—it is the rare pitcher today who breaks double figures in that category during a season. As recently as 1972, Steve Carlton completed 30 games, but today, entire pitching staffs don't even reach that total.

Today's pitchers are also on pitch counts. And fewer pitches translates into fewer decisions. While the hurlers of yesteryear regularly exceeded 200 tosses in a game—Spahn once confided that he sometimes reached 250—it is considered a good day's work now if a moundsman makes it to 100. In fact, if a pitcher today manages to last six innings, he is celebrated for his "quality" effort.

The six-inning starter, of course, is the offspring of the modern bullpen, with its closers, setup men, one-batter specialists, long relievers, and whoever else can find a spot on the bloated pitching brigades of today. As valuable as they have become, relief pitchers have generally reduced the number of wins (and losses) that starters used to accumulate.

Another more subtle change that works against pitchers has surfaced. To some extent, pitching has always been the sacrificial lamb of baseball. Although pitchers usually find ways to overcome obstacles placed before them, often over the years when they became too effective, legislation was initiated to knock them down a peg. Their mounds were moved back, and back again, the spitball and the use of other foreign substances were outlawed, and eventually even knockdown pitches were for all practical purposes removed from a hurler's bag of tricks.

At some point toward the later part of the 20th century, the powers that run baseball decided that fans come to ball parks to see hitters, not pitchers. A high-scoring game with lots of hitting, they theorized, has more appeal than a well-pitched, low-scoring game. Fans want to see home runs, it was concluded, and the more that are hit, the better they like it.

To insure this assumption, a number of changes that gave hitters the advantage were instituted. Pitching mounds were lowered, strike zones were reduced, livelier balls were put into play, and outfield fences were shortened. Combining with the limitations that these restraints placed on good pitching were inconsistent—and often atrocious—umpiring, catchers with so little experience that they didn't have a clue about calling games, and the sizeable influx in the majors of Double-A and Triple-A pitchers who usurped the playing time of bona fide big league hurlers. The net effect was that hitting proliferated, resulting in higher batting averages, more home runs, and ultimately higher scores. And pitchers bore the burden; their effectiveness diminished and their records suffered.

While the ranks of 500 home run hitters and 3,000-hit batters will continue to expand, it has reached the point now where many baseball experts are convinced that other than a few possibilities there will never be another 300-game winner. Some cite the reasons above; others have additional theories.

"It's just not important any more," said Don Sutton, the next to last hurler to accomplish the feat when he did it in 1986. "Pitchers are not willing to make the sacrifice. They don't want to stick around until they're 40. They make millions of dollars, and they can retire at 35, so why keep pitching? Why spend from mid-February to October away from home much of the time if you already have millions of dollars in the bank? I doubt very seriously that (after the next few years) there will be another 300-game winner."

Another doubter is Paul Owens, who has spent more than one-half century in baseball, most notably as the astute general manager who in the 1970s and early 1980s put together the best era in Philadelphia Phillies history. "Pretty soon, I'll never see it happen again, and I don't think anybody else will in the 21st century," said Owens. "The way they're used today, pitchers are content to go four or five or six innings, then you go to your bullpen. A starter loses a lot of potential wins that way."

This is not the first time the 300-game winner has been consigned to extinction. In the 36 years between 1888 and 1924, 11 pitchers reached that exalted level. But after Grover Cleveland Alexander won his 300th in 1924, it appeared that the species had vanished. Seventeen years elapsed before the next pitcher (Lefty Grove) won 300 games. Then 20 years passed before another 300-game winner (Spahn) came along in 1961. Soon afterward, there was a 19-year gap between the 300th wins of Early Wynn in 1963 and Gaylord Perry in 1982. During each lengthy interval, the 300-game winner was generally thought to have disappeared forever.

Perry, however, led a parade of six 300-game winners over a nine-year period. During that time, a few other hurlers, such as Tommy John with 288 wins, Bert Blyleven with 287, Ferguson Jenkins with 284, and Jim Kaat with 283, also got close. But now, the last 300-game winner was in 1990 when Nolan Ryan joined the select group.

Mel Stottlemyre, the pitching coach of the New York Yankees and a 164-game winner during an 11-year career, allows for the slim possibility that other 300-game winners could surface, but leans more toward the notion that such pitchers are a dying breed.

"It will become harder and harder," he said. "Pitching has become tougher and more demanding, and it's harder to throw consistently for as long a period as it would take to win 300 games. It would take a tremendous amount of dedication to do that. You have to have a long career and be successful every year, stay in condition all year, and stay away from injuries. I'm not sure there will be many more 300-game winners, but then again you never know.

Someone may pop up in the future with the dedication and pride that it takes to win that many games."

Although the deck seems clearly stacked against future 300-game winners, some others still have hope. One strong believer in the likelihood that the species has not become extinct is Orel Hershiser, who won 204 games himself during a fine 17-year career in the big leagues.

Hershiser claims there will be more than a few future 300-game winners, "for sure." His reasoning? "I think athletes in general always continue to progress," he said. "Just because pitching is getting really hard, it doesn't mean someone can't do it. I also don't think people retire because they have enough money. Actually, money might be an incentive for staying around longer. Another thing to consider is that a lot of young pitchers are getting an earlier start. They're pitching in the major leagues when they're 20 or 21 whereas 20 or 30 years ago, they might still be in the minors for another four or five years. So, they have more years to pitch and to win games."

Aside from the possibility that some unknown may be lurking in the shadows, ready to mount a campaign to win 300, the only likely choices to join the ranks of baseball's winningest pitchers come in the form of Roger Clemens and Greg Maddux, two of the premier pitchers of the current era. Ironically, both are throwbacks to an earlier time.

At 39 years of age, Clemens, a six-time Cy Young Award winner, entered the 2002 season with 280 career wins. The hard-throwing New York Yankees righthander has made it known that he fully expects to keep pitching for a few more years and to reach the 300 win level.

Maddux, who passed his 36th birthday early in the 2002 season, began that campaign with 257 wins. The recipient of four Cy Young awards says he thinks that the 300-game winner is a dying breed, and that the only way a pitcher can have a chance at reaching that figure is to start young, win early, and get 600 starts during his career. The Atlanta Braves pitcher isn't ready to declare himself a candidate for 300 wins.

Roger Clemens has the most wins of any active pitcher.

"It's way too far away to make it [winning 300] a goal," the masterful righthander said during the 2001 season. "As I get closer, it might be a significant goal, but I've always pitched for tomorrow and never really looked past my next start. I suppose it's possible, but I really haven't thought about it. Right now, I'm living on extra credit. The game has given me more than I ever dreamed it could."

Because he doesn't overtax his arm when he pitches and trains relentlessly, Maddux is the kind of hurler who could be on the

Greg Maddux is a strong candidate to win 300 games.

mound well into his 40s. Clemens, a physical fitness fanatic, too, could also be toeing the rubber into his 40s, despite the strain his flaming fastball puts on his arm. With both hurlers, pitching that much longer would virtually assure them of reaching 300 wins.

Are there any other candidates? Unless there is someone who has yet to come forward, the answer is a resounding no. None of the top pitchers of today is even close.

The Braves' Tom Glavine and the Arizona Diamondbacks' Randy Johnson are the only other current hurlers with 200 wins. Glavine, who's won the Cy Young Award twice, entered the 2002 season with 224, but he is a little less than one month older than Maddux. Johnson arrived at exactly 200 wins in 2001, but the four-time Cy Young Award winner began the new season as a 38-year-old. The chances of Glavine and Johnson reaching 300 wins appear slim.

Of the other active pitchers, only a few had as many as 150 wins entering the 2002 season. The list was limited to David Cone (193), Chuck Finley (189), Kevin Brown (180), Bret Saberhagen (167), David Wells (166), Mike Mussina (164), John Smoltz (160), Jamie Moyer (151), and Andy Benes (150). As the 2002 season began, Cone, Finley, and Moyer were 39 years old, Saberhagen and Wells were 38, Brown was 37, Smoltz and Benes were 34, and Mussina was 33. Some in this group were about to retire. For the others, not only was 300 wins an impossible task, but even reaching the 200-win mark was not likely for all but a few. After this group, no one else is even remotely close to 300 wins, much less 200.

That means that the burden of keeping the breed alive falls on Clemens and Maddux. Barring the unforeseen, each should reach 300. But given the current conditions involving pitchers, they could very well be the last ones to do it. And if that's the case, it will sadly be the end of one of the rarest and most noteworthy accomplishments in baseball.

Photo Credits

National Baseball Hall of Fame Library, Cooperstown, N.Y.
    Pages 2, 10, 18, 26, 34, 42, 50, 70, 72, 88, 108, 110, 118, 121,
    148, 160, 171, 178, 180

Urban Archives, Temple University, Philadelphia, Pa.
    Pages 131, 151

Courtesy of Rich Westcott
    Pages 60, 61, 78, 81, 91, 138, 140

Courtesy of George Sullivan
    Pages 51, 98

Philadelphia Athletics Historical Society
    Page 101

Seattle Mariners
    Page 128

New York Yankees
    Pages 158, 192

California Angels
    Page 168

Atlanta Braves, © Chris Hamilton 2000
    Page 193

About the Author

Rich Westcott has some idea of what it's like to stand on the mound and face an opposing hitter, having been a pitcher himself before it became apparent that his fingers were more useful pounding keyboards than gripping baseballs. Westcott has authored 11 other books during a career that has covered 40 years as a writer and editor with newspapers and magazines mostly in the Philadelphia area. He is the founder and for 14 years served as editor and publisher of *Phillies Report.* Westcott resides in Springfield, Pennsylvania.